QUIZ WHIZ 5

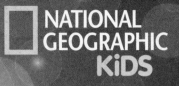

QUIZ WHIZ 5

1,000 SUPER FUN MIND-BENDING TOTALLY AWESOME TRIVIA QUESTIONS

NATIONAL GEOGRAPHIC

WASHINGTON, D.C.

Table of CONTENTS

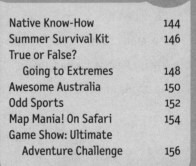

INTRODUCTION

Enter the world of Quiz Whizzers! Test your general knowledge on more than 1,000 questions and tally your score to find out if you reached a brainbox peak or hit rock bottom. Pit your wits against our in-*quiz*-itors as they challenge you on facts and figures about animals, geography, nature, history, science, pop culture, math, and amazing adventures. Discover awesome places, learn about incredible feats and natural wonders, and be amazed by science and technology.

Quiz Whiz 5 is a treasure trove of did-you-know, record-breaking, and weird, quirky, and unusual facts and statements. They are fascinating and fun, wild and wacky. There are hundreds of questions that are either true or false or multiple choice. Do you know the names of the main characters in the Harry Potter and Despicable Me movies? How many toes does a sheep have? What is a fez, a *sfouf*, a *Parcheesi*? Why is the dog Laika famous? You'll discover the answers to these questions and many more by the end of this book.

The book contains a mix of quiz games. "True or False?" quizzes have 30 theme-related random statements for you to guess which are fact or fiction. "Map Mania!" quizzes test your knowledge about people, places, and animals from around the world and include a map with locations for you to identify. Multiple-choice questions throughout the book cover movie and TV celebrities, ancient wonders, dangerous animals, heroic deeds, great adventures, food, inventions, and weird sports and activities. Each chapter ends with a "Game Show," where you'll find special photo questions and an extra-challenging "Ultimate Brain Buster."

You can work through the book on your own or challenge family and friends to a *Quiz Whiz* competition. The answers to all the questions are at the end of the book. As you tally your scores for each chapter, read the hints and tips for different ranges to help you learn more. Don't expect to get all the answers correct—the object is to have fun and learn new things. You can even revisit the book a few months later and see how your scores have improved.

Your brain has millions of interconnecting cells that constantly pass messages back and forth. As you learn new things, new connections are made or reinforced, strengthening your knowledge. Exercise those cells by working through *Quiz Whiz* and feel the energizing power of knowledge. Remembering the answers and learning new things is the name of the game.

LION CUBS,
KALAHARI DESERT

On the FARM

1 True or false?
Chickens can fly.

2 Gas released from cow farts and burps make which problem worse?
a. world hunger
b. global warming
c. noise pollution
d. mad cow disease

3 Which farm animal lives in the wild on the U.S. Virgin Islands?
a. chicken
b. donkey
c. goat
d. all of the above

CHICKEN

4 How many toes does a sheep have?
a. 1
b. 2
c. 4
d. 12

SHEEP

5 What is the name for a male goose?
a. goose-man
b. gary
c. gander
d. bull

6 If a pig stays out too long in the hot sun, it might _____.
a. get a sunburn
b. turn purple
c. go blind
d. lose its hair

PIG

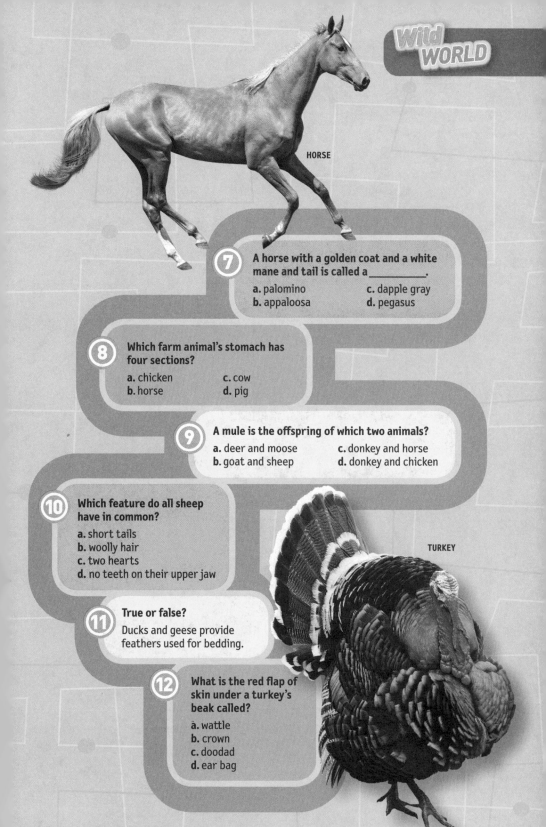

HORSE

7 A horse with a golden coat and a white mane and tail is called a _____.
a. palomino   **c.** dapple gray
b. appaloosa   **d.** pegasus

8 Which farm animal's stomach has four sections?
a. chicken   **c.** cow
b. horse   **d.** pig

9 A mule is the offspring of which two animals?
a. deer and moose   **c.** donkey and horse
b. goat and sheep   **d.** donkey and chicken

10 Which feature do all sheep have in common?
a. short tails
b. woolly hair
c. two hearts
d. no teeth on their upper jaw

TURKEY

11 True or false?
Ducks and geese provide feathers used for bedding.

12 What is the red flap of skin under a turkey's beak called?
a. wattle
b. crown
c. doodad
d. ear bag

CHECK YOUR ANSWERS ON PAGES 158–159.

CALL OF THE WILD

1 How do **scientists** track wolf populations?
a. attach radio collars
b. record howls
c. follow prints
d. all of the above

2 True or false? Cheetahs can **chirp** like a bird.

3 Which of these birds can't learn to say human words?
a. mynah bird
b. crow
c. green parrot
d. hummingbird

4 What sound does a **chimpanzee** make when it finds food?
a. whistle
b. sneeze
c. grunt
d. scream

5 **Ants** send messages to one another by _____ .
a. leaving smelly trails
b. moving small rocks
c. squeaking
d. dancing

6 When on lookout, what does a meerkat do when a jackal approaches?
a. run away
b. attack
c. squeak
d. sing "Hakuna Matata"

7 Which animal changes color to show off its **fighting** ability?
a. tiger
b. tarantula
c. chameleon
d. shark

8 True or false? You can identify a firefly species by the pattern of its flash.

9 **If a gorilla sticks out its tongue, what emotion is it expressing?**

a. anger
b. boredom
c. tiredness
d. hunger

10 **Which creature's mating calls also attract hungry bats?**

a. blue jay
b. túngara frog
c. salmon
d. mountain lion

11 **True or false? Some scientists can speak dolphin language.**

12 **What does it mean when kangaroos thump their hind legs?**

a. rain is coming
b. danger is near
c. they see food
d. disco music is playing

13 **Fox calls sound like _____.**

a. a high-pitched bark
b. nothing; foxes are silent
c. a piglike grunt
d. a meow

14 **Which ape can learn sign language?**

a. gorilla
b. chimpanzee
c. orangutan
d. all of the above

15 **True or false? Birds make up new calls every time they sing.**

WOLF

CHECK YOUR ANSWERS ON PAGES 158–159.

WHAT A HOOT!

1 Which critter would make a yummy dinner for an owl?
a. mouse
b. skunk
c. spider
d. all of the above

2 Owl feathers have a special shape that allows the bird to _____.
a. swim underwater
b. fly silently
c. survive forest fires
d. time travel

SNOWY OWL

3 What is the name for the sharp, pointy nails on an owl's feet?
a. talons
b. claws
c. grips
d. meathooks

4 True or false? All owls only hunt at night.

5 What objects do owls have trouble seeing?
a. faraway objects
b. running mice
c. nearby objects
d. anything in bright daylight

6 What might an owl do when it is attacked?
a. play dead
b. hiss
c. scream
d. throw poison darts

7 Where do snowy owls nest?
a. in trees
b. on high cliffs
c. on the ground
d. on ocean ice

10 Which is the smallest owl species?
a. elf owl
b. great horned owl
c. barn owl
d. snowy owl

8 True or false?
An owl has to turn its head in order to look to the side.

9 Which habitat do burrowing owls prefer?
a. the Arctic
b. rain forest
c. marsh
d. desert

12 The "horns" on a great horned owl are actually_____.
a. bony antlers
b. giant feathers
c. poisonous spikes
d. tufted ears

11 Short-eared owls don't live on which continent?
a. Australia
b. North America
c. Asia
d. Europe

13 When hiking in the woods, you may come across an owl pellet. What is it?
a. owl poop
b. owl vomit, or coughed-up food
c. an egg
d. a ball of soft feathers

14 What is the name of Harry Potter's snowy owl?
a. Snowy
b. Hedwig
c. Pigwidgeon
d. Wilbur

15 True or false?
Baby owls are called owlings.

CHECK YOUR ANSWERS ON PAGES 158–159.

TIME FOR A CHANGE

1 Damselflies—like many other animals—shed their old skin as they grow. What is this process called?

a. bursting
b. powering up
c. molting
d. skin shifting

2 Which **feature** disappears as a tadpole transforms into a frog?

a. a long tail
b. legs
c. scales
d. wings

4 Which step happens first to a **caterpillar** inside a cocoon?

a. It grows wings.
b. It dissolves into goo.
c. Its eyes get bigger.
d. Its legs fall off.

3 True or false? As a **flounder** grows, an eye **moves** from one side of its head to the other.

6 Which Arctic animal turns white in the winter?

a. Arctic fox
b. Arctic hare
c. collared lemming
d. all of the above

5 Which animal is born with white "puppy" fur, which it casts off three weeks after birth?

a. giraffe
b. gray seal
c. dolphin
d. rabbit

8 In cold areas, how long may it take for a tadpole to become a **bullfrog**?

a. 2 days
b. 8 weeks
c. 3 years
d. 10 years

7 How often do reindeer **grow** new antlers?

a. every few months
b. once a year
c. every five years
d. they never do

9 **True or false?** A dog with all its fur **shaved off** will be more comfortable on hot days.

10 **How can you tell when a snake is about to shed its skin?**
a. Its eyes get cloudy.
b. It climbs high up in a tree.
c. It gets purple spots.
d. It starts squealing.

11 **What is a butterfly's cocoon made out of?**
a. wood
b. leaves
c. glass
d. silk

RED DAMSELFLY EMERGES FROM ITS OLD SKIN

12 **True or false?** Every year, **penguins** grow a new set of feathers. When this happens, they don't eat for two to three weeks.

13 **What does a tarantula do before shedding its exoskeleton?**
a. flips on its back
b. eats more than usual
c. chews on rocks
d. dances a jig

14 **Which animal needs to find new, empty shells to move into as it grows?**
a. scorpion
b. turtle
c. hermit crab
d. lobster

15 **Which sea creature can quickly change color?**
a. shark
b. moray eel
c. octopus
d. tuna fish

CHECK YOUR ANSWERS ON PAGES 158–159.

PURRFECT Cats

MOUNTAIN LION

1 Which of the following is not another name for a mountain lion?

a. cougar
b. catamount
c. puma
d. jalopy

2 What do you call a group of lions?

a. a pride
b. a meeting
c. an army
d. a circus

3 Which wild cat can hang upside-down from a tree branch?

a. clouded leopard
b. cheetah
c. Bengal tiger
d. African lion

4 Jaguars hunt caiman in the water. A caiman is similar to _____.

a. a chicken
b. a moose
c. an alligator
d. a zebra

5 Which cat has large paws that act like snowshoes in winter?

a. lion
b. lynx
c. panther
d. ocelot

SPOTTED LEOPARD CUB

6 Why do many wild cats have spots or stripes?

a. to stand out
b. to help them hide
c. to send messages
d. to attract people

JAGUAR

7 True or false? All wild cats eat only meat.

8 If you're an antelope in Africa, which cat do you need to watch out for?
a. leopard   c. mountain lion
b. jaguar   d. lynx

9 Which is the world's largest wild cat?
a. mountain lion   c. cheetah
b. leopard   d. Siberian tiger

10 For how long does a cheetah usually run during a hunt?
a. less than a minute   c. about half an hour
b. 5 to 10 minutes   d. more than an hour

CHEETAH

11 Which of these is a species of tiger?
a. Indonesian
b. African
c. Sumatran
d. all of the above

A GROUP OF WILD LIONS

12 True or false? Lions live in the wild only in Africa.

13 What could you wear on the back of your head to help prevent a tiger attack?
a. perfume
b. bug spray
c. a striped bandana
d. a face mask

CHECK YOUR ANSWERS ON PAGES 158–159.

MAP MANIA!
ANIMAL INVADERS

Invasive species are animals and plants that don't naturally belong. They come from a different place, and, in certain areas, they harm the local animals and plants.

NORTH AMERICA
6
2
ATLANTIC OCEAN
4
PACIFIC OCEAN
SOUTH AMERICA
ANTARCTICA

① EUROPEAN RABBIT

What was supposed to keep invasive rabbits away from farmland?

a. wild tigers
b. giant noisemakers
c. a 2,000-mile (3,219-km)-long fence
d. a spray with a disgusting scent

② BOA CONSTRICTOR

How did these invasive snakes likely end up in their new home?

a. They swam across the ocean.
b. Pet snakes escaped.
c. An attacking army brought them.
d. A hurricane carried them.

③ LONG-TAILED MACAQUE

What type of animal does this monkey compete with for fruit and seeds?

a. fish
b. frogs
c. tigers
d. birds

④ MONGOOSE

True or false? Farmers released mongooses on purpose to hunt rats.

ARCTIC OCEAN

EUROPE

ASIA

AFRICA

PACIFIC OCEAN

3

INDIAN OCEAN

5

1

⑤ MALLARD DUCK

Invasive mallard ducks often have babies with native ducks, such as the African black duck. Why is this a problem?

a. Mallard ducks are poisonous.
b. Native snakes eat the eggs.
c. Native ducks could disappear.
d. The babies aren't healthy.

⑥ ZEBRA MUSSELS

What is the best way to keep zebra mussels from invading more lakes?

a. send lionfish to eat them
b. wash off boats when they attach
c. build fences around lakes
d. serve them in restaurants

7–12 MATCH EACH ANIMAL WITH THE AREA IT HAS INVADED SHOWN IN ORANGE ON THE MAP.

CHECK YOUR ANSWERS ON PAGES 158–159.

THE ICE AGE

1 During the Ice Age, where could you find large **cave lions?**

a. America
b. Europe
c. Asia
d. all of the above

2 True or false?
Mammoth and mastodon are two words for the same large elephant-like creature.

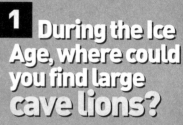

WOOLLY MAMMOTH

3 Which is the common name for a **wolf** from the Ice Age?

a. mega wolf
b. werewolf
c. dire wolf
d. wolfemania

4 When people talk about the Ice Age, they usually mean a period that lasted for about 10,000 years and was coldest _____.

a. before Earth existed
b. about 21,000 years ago
c. about 500 years ago
d. during the summer

5 What is the name of the squirrel-like creature from the movie *Ice Age?*

a. Snowball
b. Goofy
c. Scrat
d. Pipsqueak

6 True or false?
During the Ice Age, the entire planet was covered with ice.

7 The Irish elk, a giant deer, had **antlers** that could grow as wide as which of the following is long?

a. a banana
b. a hockey stick
c. a kayak
d. a school bus

8 In the movie *Ice Age*, which of these animals is not a main character?

a. Carl the cave lion
b. Diego the saber-toothed cat
c. Sid the sloth
d. Manny the woolly mammoth

9 How many omelets could you make from one **elephant bird egg**?

a. 3
b. 50
c. 1,000
d. a million

10 The **glyptodont** had an armored shell and was closely related to which animal?

a. armadillo
b. turtle
c. dolphin
d. mosquito

11 True or false? Camels lived during the Ice Age.

12 Which modern animal is closest in size to the extinct giant beaver?

a. wolf
b. black bear
c. elephant
d. blue whale

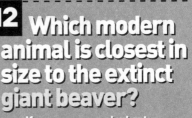

13 Which **Ice Age** animal still lives in the wild today?

a. mastodon
b. musk ox
c. woolly mammoth
d. dodo bird

14 A giant sloth's **claws** were as long as which of the following?

a. a pencil
b. a person's foot
c. a person's arm
d. a full-grown alligator

15 True or false? Humans **hunted** woolly mammoths.

HIP HOPPER

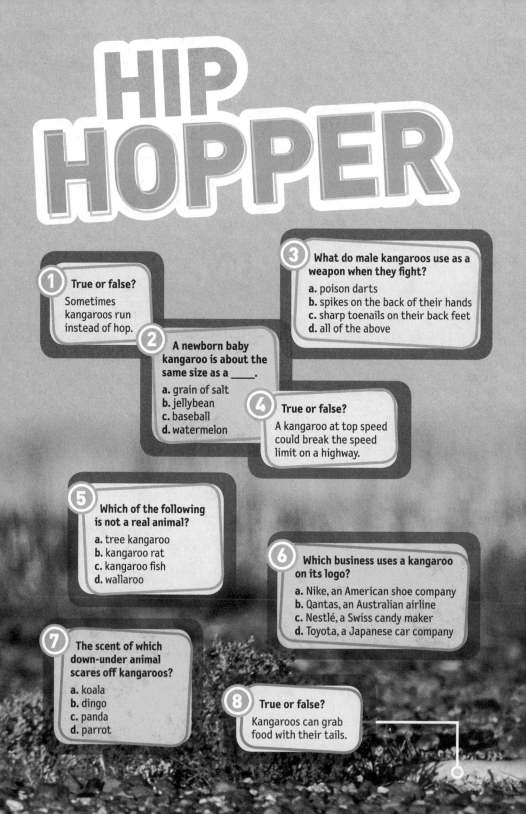

1 **True or false?**
Sometimes kangaroos run instead of hop.

2 A newborn baby kangaroo is about the same size as a ____.
a. grain of salt
b. jellybean
c. baseball
d. watermelon

3 What do male kangaroos use as a weapon when they fight?
a. poison darts
b. spikes on the back of their hands
c. sharp toenails on their back feet
d. all of the above

4 **True or false?**
A kangaroo at top speed could break the speed limit on a highway.

5 Which of the following is not a real animal?
a. tree kangaroo
b. kangaroo rat
c. kangaroo fish
d. wallaroo

6 Which business uses a kangaroo on its logo?
a. Nike, an American shoe company
b. Qantas, an Australian airline
c. Nestlé, a Swiss candy maker
d. Toyota, a Japanese car company

7 The scent of which down-under animal scares off kangaroos?
a. koala
b. dingo
c. panda
d. parrot

8 **True or false?**
Kangaroos can grab food with their tails.

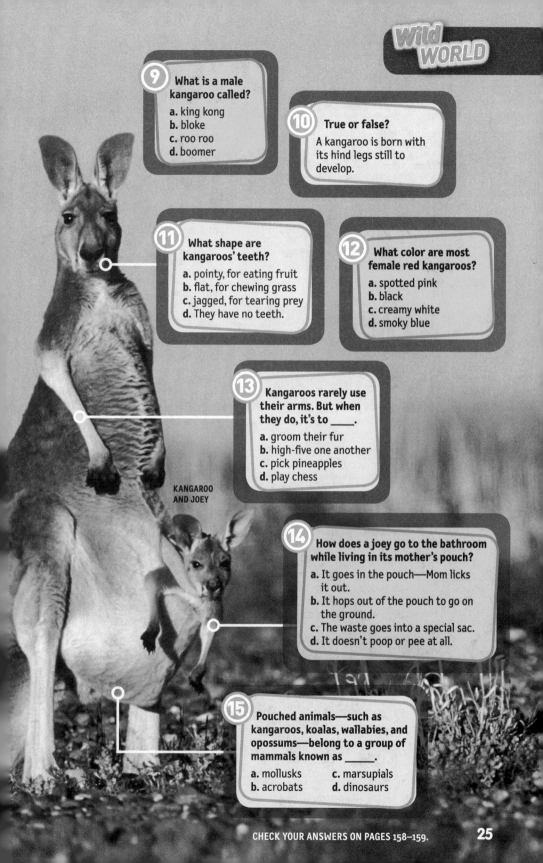

9 What is a male kangaroo called?

a. king kong
b. bloke
c. roo roo
d. boomer

10 True or false?
A kangaroo is born with its hind legs still to develop.

11 What shape are kangaroos' teeth?

a. pointy, for eating fruit
b. flat, for chewing grass
c. jagged, for tearing prey
d. They have no teeth.

12 What color are most female red kangaroos?

a. spotted pink
b. black
c. creamy white
d. smoky blue

13 Kangaroos rarely use their arms. But when they do, it's to _____.

a. groom their fur
b. high-five one another
c. pick pineapples
d. play chess

KANGAROO AND JOEY

14 How does a joey go to the bathroom while living in its mother's pouch?

a. It goes in the pouch—Mom licks it out.
b. It hops out of the pouch to go on the ground.
c. The waste goes into a special sac.
d. It doesn't poop or pee at all.

15 Pouched animals—such as kangaroos, koalas, wallabies, and opossums—belong to a group of mammals known as _____.

a. mollusks
b. acrobats
c. marsupials
d. dinosaurs

CHECK YOUR ANSWERS ON PAGES 158–159.

Animal ARCHITECTS

BEAVER HOUSE

1 What do you call the house made of sticks that beavers build?

a. lodge
b. sticktopia
c. teepee
d. beaver world

2 What shape is each cell in a wasp's nest?

a. square
b. circle
c. hexagon
d. triangle

WASP

3 Which animal constructs a system of underground burrows?

a. sloth
b. prairie dog
c. tortoise
d. flamingo

4 Bees produce _____ to help build their hives.

a. glue
b. silk
c. wax
d. chocolate

BEE

5 Fire ants cross a stream by _____.

a. flying over one at a time
b. forming a raft made of their own bodies
c. building a bridge out of sticks
d. digging a tunnel under the stream

6 Which crafty African animal built this gigantic nest?

a. social weaver bird
b. olive baboon
c. leopard
d. hornbill

GIGANTIC NEST

26

7 **True or false?** Cathedral termites can build a mound that is taller than an elephant.

8 **True or false?** Some spiders' webs can withstand hurricane-force winds.

SPIDER

9 **Which bird lays its eggs in a burrow instead of a nest?**

a. flamingo
b. crow
c. ostrich
d. puffin

10 **Where do swallows regularly build their mud nests?**

a. in trees
b. on the ground
c. on rocks by the ocean
d. attached to buildings

11 **In one year, about how much will a coral colony on a reef grow?**

a. less than 1 inch (2.5 cm)
c. about 2 feet (61 cm)
b. about 10 inches (25 cm)
d. more than 3 feet (91 cm)

CHIMPANZEE

12 **True or false?** Every night, chimpanzees build—high in trees—a new nest to sleep in.

TRUE or FALSE?
It's a Jungle

1. ALL MONKEYS HAVE LONG TAILS.

2. TIGERS LIVE IN THE JUNGLES OF SOUTH AMERICA.

3. YOU COULD FIND 200 DIFFERENT SPECIES OF ANTS ON A SINGLE TREE IN A RAIN FOREST.

4. ALL SPECIES OF LEMURS LIVING IN MADAGASCAR ARE IN DANGER OF GOING EXTINCT.

5. THE OKAPI IS A STRIPED ANIMAL RELATED TO THE GIRAFFE.

6. THE WORLD'S LARGEST RAIN FOREST IS IN INDIA.

7. A DEADLY FUNGUS HAS KILLED MANY JUNGLE FROGS AROUND THE WORLD.

8. MORE THAN HALF OF THE WORLD'S PLANT AND ANIMAL SPECIES LIVE IN TROPICAL RAIN FORESTS.

9. AN ORCHID IS A COLORFUL JUNGLE BIRD.

10. THE AMAZON RAIN FOREST IS GETTING LESS RAIN THAN IT USED TO.

11. JAGUARS ARE POWERFUL SWIMMERS.

12. SOME RAIN FOREST ANIMALS LIVE THEIR WHOLE LIVES IN THE TREETOPS HIGH ABOVE THE GROUND.

13. THERE ARE NO RAIN FORESTS IN AFRICA.

14. THE QUETZAL IS A BAT THAT EATS TROPICAL FRUIT.

15. SKUNKS LIVE IN THE RAIN FOREST IN SOUTH AMERICA.

16 GREEN TREE PYTHONS HAVE YELLOW AND RED BABIES.

17 ONE KIND OF SPECIALTY COFFEE IS MADE FROM BEANS FOUND IN THE POOP OF A RAIN FOREST ANIMAL.

18 SLOTHS ARE A TYPE OF MONKEY.

19 CUTTING DOWN THE RAIN FOREST CAUSES SOME ANIMALS AND PLANTS TO GO EXTINCT.

20 PINEAPPLES GROW ON TREES IN THE RAIN FOREST.

21 ASIAN ELEPHANTS LIVE IN JUNGLES.

22 A PARROT IN THE WILD MAY LIVE TO THE AGE OF 80.

23 SPIDER MONKEYS LIKE TO EAT SPIDERS.

24 SOME RAIN FOREST BATS DRINK FLOWER NECTAR.

25 ALL BRIGHTLY COLORED FROGS ARE POISONOUS.

26 AUSTRALIAN RAIN FORESTS CONTAIN PLANTS RELATED TO THOSE THAT GREW AT THE TIME WHEN DINOSAURS EXISTED.

27 A TOUCAN'S BEAK IS LONGER THAN ITS BODY.

28 THE BORNEO RAIN FOREST IS HOME TO PYGMY ELEPHANTS THE SIZE OF HOUSE CATS.

29 IF YOU REACH INTO A WATER-FILLED HOLE IN A RAIN FOREST TREE, YOU MAY FIND A CRAB!

30 THE BOA CONSTRICTOR IS THE LONGEST SNAKE IN THE WORLD.

CHECK YOUR ANSWERS ON PAGES 158–159.

GAME SHOW

ULTIMATE ANIMAL CHALLENGE

1 How many hot dogs could a hungry tiger eat in one night?

a. less than 50   c. about 500
b. only 8   d. more than 1,000

2 TRUE OR FALSE?

Male Caribbean reef squid "talk" by changing color.

3 Which is the name of a giant bear that lived during the Ice Age?

a. short-faced bear
b. abominable bear-man
c. mega-colossal bear
d. dwarf bear

4 Which rain forest animal loves the gross-smelling flowers of the kapok tree?

a. snake   c. bat
b. monkey   d. toucan

5 What does a crab do just before shedding its old shell?

a. expands like a balloon
b. climbs a tree
c. swims to a deserted island
d. whistles a song

6 During a drought, where do red kangaroos get water?

a. the ocean
b. the grocery store
c. underground
d. from plants

7 Which wild cat hunts gazelles?

a. ocelot
b. cheetah
c. jaguar
d. lynx

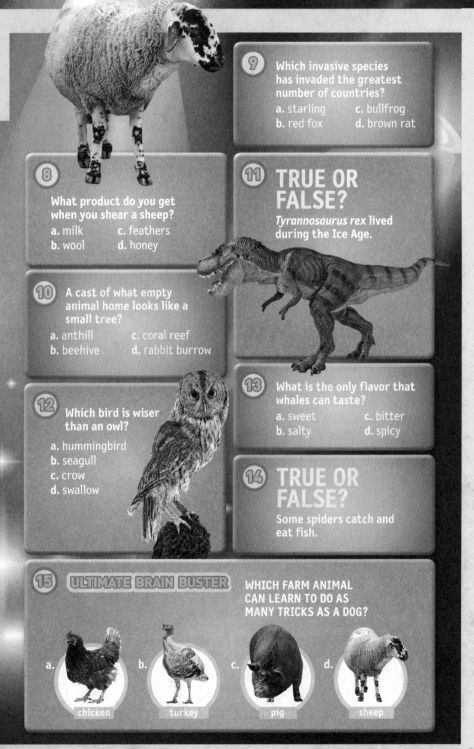

9 Which invasive species has invaded the greatest number of countries?
a. starling
c. bullfrog
b. red fox
d. brown rat

8 What product do you get when you shear a sheep?
a. milk
c. feathers
b. wool
d. honey

11 ## TRUE OR FALSE?
Tyrannosaurus rex lived during the Ice Age.

10 A cast of what empty animal home looks like a small tree?
a. anthill
c. coral reef
b. beehive
d. rabbit burrow

12 Which bird is wiser than an owl?
a. hummingbird
b. seagull
c. crow
d. swallow

13 What is the only flavor that whales can taste?
a. sweet
c. bitter
b. salty
d. spicy

14 ## TRUE OR FALSE?
Some spiders catch and eat fish.

15 ULTIMATE BRAIN BUSTER
WHICH FARM ANIMAL CAN LEARN TO DO AS MANY TRICKS AS A DOG?

a. chicken
b. turkey
c. pig
d. sheep

CHECK YOUR ANSWERS ON PAGES 158–159.

EXPLORING NIAGARA FALLS

1 Niagara Falls is one of the most popular tourist destinations in the U.S.A. and Canada. About how many people visit each year?

a. 50,000
b. 200,000
c. 5 million
d. 12 million

2 True or false? Niagara Falls State Park is the oldest state park in the U.S.A.

3 Niagara Falls is made up of three waterfalls: the American Falls, Horseshoe Falls, and _____ Falls.

a. Wedding Gown
b. Bridal Veil
c. Pocket Watch
d. Running Shoe

4 More than 6 million cubic feet (168,000 cu m) of water rush over Niagara Falls every minute. That's enough to fill about _____ bathtubs!

a. 1,000
b. 10,000
c. 100,000
d. 1 million

5 Who was the first person to travel over Niagara Falls in a barrel?

a. Annie Taylor, a school teacher from Michigan
b. Isabella Bird, an explorer from Great Britain
c. "Super Dave" Munday, a mechanic from Canada
d. George L. Statakis, a waiter from Greece

6 Why is Niagara Falls a great place to see rainbows?

a. It rains almost every day there.
b. Glass prisms are scattered around the Falls.
c. Sunshine reflects off the mist from the Falls.
d. Rainbow-colored algae living in the water glow.

7 In what year did the *Maid of the Mist* service—the boats that now bring tourists near Niagara Falls—first start?

a. 1806
b. 1846
c. 1886
d. 1906

8 Due to erosion, about how far back has Niagara Falls moved in the last 12,500 years?

a. 500 feet (152.4 m)
b. 2 miles (3.2 km)
c. 7 miles (11.3 km)
d. 500 miles (804.7 km)

9 The speed of the water going over Niagara Falls can reach up to _____.

a. 22 miles an hour (35.4 km/h)
b. 68 miles an hour (109.4 km/h)
c. 135 miles an hour (217.3 km/h)
d. 326 miles an hour (524.6 km/h)

10 True or false?

There are about ten waterfalls in the world that are "taller" than Niagara Falls.

11 The brown foam at the bottom of Niagara Falls is caused mostly by _____.

a. clay particles
b. pollution
c. animal poop
d. dead fish

12 Which of the following animals can be found living near Niagara Falls?

a. lake sturgeon
b. bald eagles
c. roadrunners
d. a and b

13 Which of the Great Lakes does *not* drain into the Niagara River?

a. Huron
b. Erie
c. Ontario
d. Michigan

14 True or false?

Niagara Falls went dry in March 1848.

CHECK YOUR ANSWERS ON PAGES 159–161.

NATION NICKNAMES

1 The Rock of Cashel fortress is in the Emerald Isle, which is the nickname for _____.

a. Malta
b. Iceland
c. Ireland
d. Greenland

2 Which grain-producing nation is known as the Breadbasket of Europe?

a. Bulgaria
b. Ukraine
c. Estonia
d. France

3 Which city is *not* in the Land Down Under?

a. Perth
b. Glasgow
c. Sydney
d. Melbourne

4 True or false? Most Mongolians live in the Land of the Blue Sky.

5 This country, whose capital city is Santiago, is known as the Land of Poets.

a. Pakistan
b. Mongolia
c. Chile
d. Spain

6 The largest city in the Land of Smiles is _____.

a. Paris, France
b. Auckland, New Zealand
c. Timbuktu, Mali
d. Bangkok, Thailand

7 Barbados is known as the Land of the Flying _____.

a. Fish
b. Parrot
c. Pig
d. Dragonfly

8 True or false? Japan is often called the Land of the Crescent Moon.

ROCK OF CASHEL

9 What large island in the Mediterranean Sea looks like it's getting kicked by the country known as The Boot?

a. Madagascar   c. Sicily
b. Ireland   d. Puerto Rico

10 Which island country is called the Teardrop of India—not only for its shape but also for its location?

a. Sri Lanka   c. Singapore
b. Maldives   d. Hokkaido

11 The Rainbow Nation hosted the FIFA World Cup in 2010. What country was that?

a. Namibia   c. Colombia
b. Poland   d. South Africa

12 Want to see active volcanoes and glacial lagoons? Visit _____, also called the Land of Fire and Ice.

a. Argentina
b. Iceland
c. Papua New Guinea
d. Honduras

13 True or false?

Vancouver, Montreal, and Yellowknife are all cities in the country known as the Great White North.

CHECK YOUR ANSWERS ON PAGES 159–161.

On the MOVE

RICKSHAW

1. There are more _____ than people in the Netherlands.
   - **a.** bicycles
   - **b.** cars
   - **c.** motorcycles
   - **d.** skateboards

2. In which city would you be most likely to travel by rickshaw?
   - **a.** Edinburgh, Scotland
   - **b.** Nuuk, Greenland
   - **c.** Quito, Ecuador
   - **d.** Beijing, China

3. What's the top speed of Japan's magnetic levitation (maglev) trains?
   - **a.** 75 miles an hour (121 km/h)
   - **b.** 150 miles an hour (241 km/h)
   - **c.** 300 miles an hour (483 km/h)
   - **d.** 600 miles an hour (966 km/h)

4. Which iconic form of public transportation travels up and down the hills of San Francisco?
   - **a.** double-decker buses
   - **b.** cable cars
   - **c.** trains
   - **d.** monorails

5. What colorful vehicles in Latin America take their name from animals sometimes brought on board?
   - **a.** turtle taxis
   - **b.** chicken buses
   - **c.** rooster railroads
   - **d.** armadillo automobiles

6. What color are most cabs in London, England?
   - **a.** blue
   - **b.** black
   - **c.** yellow
   - **d.** pink

STREETS OF SAN FRANCISCO, CALIFORNIA, U.S.A.

7 In Venice, Italy, you'll see tourists exploring the canals in which vehicle?

a. gondola   **c.** submarine
b. rubber boat   **d.** hovercraft

GRAND CANAL, VENICE, ITALY

8 Jeepneys, brightly colored vehicles made from old World War II jeeps, are a cheap and popular way to get around in _____.

a. Japan
b. Germany
c. Sweden
d. the Philippines

JEEPNEY

AN ISLAND IN THE MALDIVES

9 **True or false?** Matatus are trained camels used to transport people in North Africa.

10 **True or false?** Visitors to the Maldives often take seaplane "taxis" between the archipelago's islands.

11 **True or false?** Feluccas are vehicles with excellent shock absorbers used to navigate India's bumpy roads.

Pack Your Bags!

1 IN ALBANIA, NODDING ONE'S HEAD UP AND DOWN MEANS "NO."

2 NEW YORK CITY HAS THE MOST ROLLS ROYCE CARS PER CAPITA OF ANY CITY ON EARTH.

3 THE WORLD'S HIGHEST AIRPORT IS IN SWITZERLAND.

4 RUSSIA HAS THE LONGEST COASTLINE OF ANY COUNTRY IN THE WORLD.

5 HONOLULU, HAWAII, IS THE ONLY CITY IN THE U.S.A. WITH A ROYAL PALACE.

6 COINS FROM VATICAN CITY CANNOT BE USED IN ITALY OR THE REST OF THE EUROPEAN UNION (EU).

7 PARTS OF MEXICO CITY ARE SINKING FASTER THAN VENICE, ITALY, AS WATER LEVELS RISE.

8 THE WORLD'S STEEPEST WOODEN ROLLER COASTER IS AT CONEY ISLAND, NEW YORK CITY.

9 SINGAPORE'S CHANGI AIRPORT HAS A BUTTERFLY GARDEN.

10 THERE ARE DISNEY AMUSEMENT PARKS IN FRANCE, CHINA, AND JAPAN.

11 MORE TOURISTS VISIT PRAGUE ZOO THAN ANY OTHER ZOOLOGICAL GARDENS IN EUROPE.

12 THE WORLD'S FIRST SUBWAY OPENED IN PARIS.

13 HAWAII, U.S.A., IS HOME TO THE WORLD'S LARGEST MAZE, WHICH IS SHAPED LIKE A PINEAPPLE.

14 THERE ARE ABOUT ONE MILLION LIONS LIVING IN LAKE NAKURU NATIONAL PARK IN KENYA.

15 SAUDI ARABIA'S KING FAHD INTERNATIONAL AIRPORT IS LARGER IN AREA THAN THE NEIGHBORING COUNTRY OF BAHRAIN.

16 VISITORS TO THE DESERT CITY OF DUBAI, UNITED ARAB EMIRATES, CAN STILL TOBOGGAN, SKI, AND HAVE SNOWBALL FIGHTS.

17 IF YOU LOOKED FOR TWO MINUTES AT EACH OBJECT IN THE BRITISH MUSEUM, IT WOULD TAKE YOU FIVE YEARS TO VIEW THE ENTIRE COLLECTION.

18 VISITORS TO AUSTRALIA CAN SEE THE BIGGEST BANANA STATUE IN THE WORLD.

19 WHEN YOU'RE "GLAMPING," YOU'RE CAMPING IN LUXURY.

20 ALL OF THE AIRPLANE RUNWAYS SERVING ANTARCTICA'S MCMURDO STATION ARE PAVED OR MADE OF GRAVEL.

21 AT AN ELEPHANT-SHAPED HOTEL IN SRI LANKA, GUESTS SLEEP IN ITS BELLY.

22 NAMIBIA'S FISH RIVER CANYON IS TWICE AS BIG AS THE GRAND CANYON.

23 WHEN DINING IN CHILE, YOU SHOULDN'T EAT ANYTHING WITH YOUR HANDS— IT'S CONSIDERED RUDE!

24 A FLORIDA, U.S.A., WATER PARK HAS A SUPER-LOOP WATERSLIDE CALLED THE WEDGIE.

25 LONDON WAS THE WORLD'S MOST POPULAR DESTINATION FOR FOREIGN TOURISTS IN 2013.

26 SERENGETI NATIONAL PARK IS THE OLDEST NATIONAL PARK IN THE WORLD.

27 YOU CAN GO GOLFING NEAR THE RUNWAY AT HONG KONG INTERNATIONAL AIRPORT.

28 VISITORS TO GUATEMALA'S TIKAL NATIONAL PARK REGULARLY SEE SUN BEARS AND ORANGUTANS.

29 THE MUSEUM OF CLEAN IN IDAHO HAS COLLECTIONS OF TOILETS, TUBS, AND VACUUM CLEANERS.

30 ABOUT 2.6 MILLION HOTEL ROOMS ARE RENTED FOR USE EVERY DAY IN THE U.S.A.

Sweet TREATS

PAVLOVA

1. Australians love pavlova, a meringue-based cake. It's named after a famous Russian _____.

a. gymnast
b. ballerina
c. high-jumper
d. soccer player

2. **True or false?** People in Japan can choose scoops of eel-, cherry-blossom-, or soy-chicken-flavored ice cream.

CHERRY BLOSSOM

3. *Churchkhela* are a favorite dessert of people in the Eastern European country of Georgia. What are they?

a. pies made of peaches and pine nuts
b. donuts with sour cream filling
c. rhubarb-flavored hard candies
d. nuts dipped in concentrated grape juice

4. Eating shortbread on Hogmanay (New Year's Eve) is a tradition in which country?

a. Chile
b. Norway
c. Scotland
d. New Zealand

5. You'd be most likely to enjoy the honey-and-walnut-laden dessert called baklava at a café in which city?

a. Athens, Greece
b. Beijing, China
c. Mexico City, Mexico
d. Copenhagen, Denmark

BAKLAVA

6 **True or false?** Some Asian candy shops sell red sesame-, grilled-lamb-, red-bean-, or jellyfish-flavored caramels.

7 **If you ordered Sachertorte at Vienna's Sacher Hotel, what kind of dessert would you get?**

a. a lemon cupcake with cream cheese frosting
b. a cream puff with raspberry sauce
c. a chocolate cake with apricot glaze or jam
d. a cinnamon-sugar cookie

SACHER HOTEL, VIENNA, AUSTRIA

8 **Gelato, *dondurma*, and *kulfi* are all types of what?**

a. ice cream
b. brownies
c. candy bars
d. cookies

DULCE DE LECHE

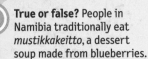

9 **Which country celebrates *dulce de leche* day on June 21, in honor of its traditional caramel dessert?**

a. Bolivia
b. Uruguay
c. Brazil
d. Argentina

10 **People in Lebanon enjoy a yellow almond cake called *sfouf* for dessert. What spice gives it a yellow hue?**

a. cinnamon
b. vanilla
c. turmeric
d. cloves

11 **True or false?** People in Namibia traditionally eat *mustikkakeitto*, a dessert soup made from blueberries.

MUSTIKKAKEITTO SOUP

IT'S THE LAW!

1 There is no speed limit on about half of the highways in which country?

a. Switzerland
b. Germany
c. Japan
d. Botswana

2 Women are not allowed to drive in _____.

a. Bhutan
b. Fiji
c. Saudi Arabia
d. Tanzania

3 True or false? It's illegal to eat or drink anything while driving in Cyprus.

4 In many countries it is against the law to do what to money?

a. photograph it
b. destroy it
c. spend it
d. eat it

5 In which of these cities is feeding pigeons illegal?

a. San Francisco, California, U.S.A.
b. Venice, Italy
c. Lausanne, Switzerland
d. all of the above

6 It's against the law to wear _____ away from the beachfront in Barcelona, Spain.

a. floppy hats
b. bikinis
c. sunglasses
d. flip-flops

7 True or false? It's illegal to drive while blindfolded in Alabama, U.S.A.

8 It's illegal to chew gum on the public transit trains in which city?

a. Washington, D.C., U.S.A.
b. Dubai, United Arab Emirates
c. Singapore, Singapore
d. all of the above

9 It's illegal to eat on the steps of a _____ in Florence, Italy.

a. restaurant
b. private home
c. church
d. department store

10 In Rwanda it's illegal to take pictures of what?

a. artwork
b. government buildings
c. fireworks
d. animals

11 Which of the following items is it illegal to import into Nigeria?

a. mineral water
b. soft drinks
c. eggs
d. all of the above

12 True or false? It's illegal to kiss in public in Dubai.

13 In Barbados, it's illegal to wear clothes with which pattern?

a. plaid
b. polka-dots
c. camouflage
d. stripes

U.S. DESERT HIGHWAY

CHECK YOUR ANSWERS ON PAGES 159–161.

On Your MARKS

SACK OF COAL

1 Where in the world can people participate in the nighttime Midnight Sun Run in full daylight?

a. London, England   **c.** Moscow, Russia
b. Reykjavik, Iceland   **d.** Nairobi, Kenya

2 During the wild 90-second-long "Il Palio," people ride _____ through the heart of Siena, Italy.

a. horses
b. bulls
c. llamas
d. porcupines

3 **True or false?** Competitors at the World Coal Carrying Championships race carrying a sack of coal on their shoulders.

PORCUPINE

4 The southernmost race in the world is the Antarctica Ice Marathon. What is the average temperature at this event?

a. −4°F (−20°C)
b. −15°F (−26°C)
c. −30°F (−34°C)
d. −60°F (−51°C)

5 At the Run for Your Lives 5K race, competitors are chased by what?

a. people dressed as zombies
b. bulls
c. dogs
d. food-throwing spectators

6 Competitors at the Jungle Marathon sleep in strung-up hammocks between each stage of the race. Where does this event take place?

a. Gabon's Congo rain forest
b. China's Da Hinggan forest
c. Italy's Alps
d. Brazil's Amazon rain forest

ANTARCTICA ICE MARATHON

7 Which mode of transportation is *not* used in the 4,970-mile (7,998-km) Dakar Rally race through rugged parts of South America?

a. motorcycle
b. four-wheeler
c. truck
d. jet ski

MINI COOPER ON THE DAKAR RALLY

8 At the Ducktona 500 in Sheboygan Falls, Wisconsin, U.S.A., thousands of what race down the Sheboygan River?

a. rolls of duct tape
b. live ducks
c. plastic ducks
d. duck boat models

9 People from around the world come to Castletown Harbour in the Isle of Man (between Great Britain and Ireland) to race in what?

a. dragon boats
b. inner tubes
c. tin bathtubs
d. animal-shaped inflatables

10 San Diego, California, U.S.A., hosts a surfing competition where _____ are judged on how long they ride the waves.

a. cats
b. dogs
c. turtles
d. iguanas

11 **True or false?** Competitors in the Wife-Carrying World Championships race 273 yards (249.6 m) over hurdles and through a pool—while carrying their wives.

WIFE-CARRYING COMPETITION

CHECK YOUR ANSWERS ON PAGES 159–161.

MAP MANIA!
FLAGS OF THE WORLD

Unscramble the names of the
countries that these flags
belong to.

1 DSABBORA

2 DCANAA

3 YAGUNA

4 RORANDA

5 TAAIVL

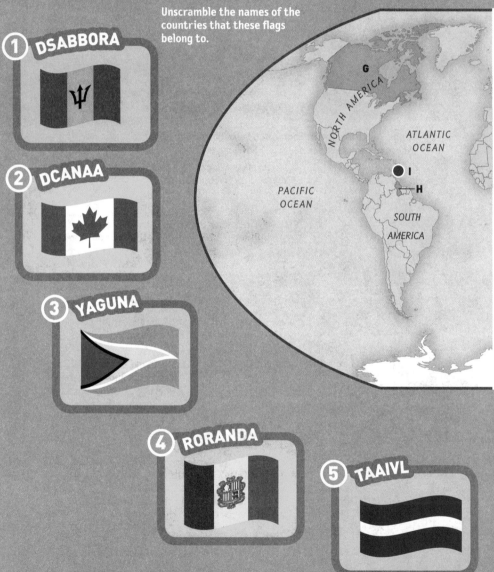

NORTH AMERICA

G

ATLANTIC
OCEAN

PACIFIC
OCEAN

I

H

SOUTH
AMERICA

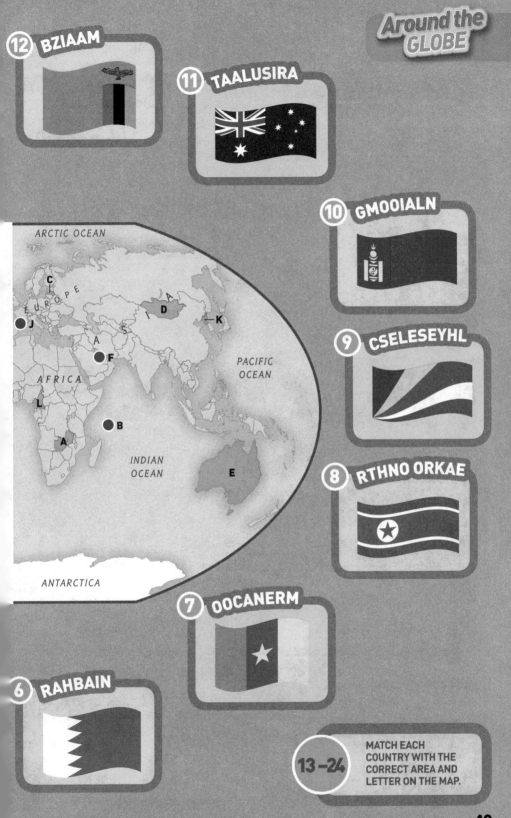

12 BZIAAM

11 TAALUSIRA

10 GMOOIALN

9 CSELESEYHL

8 RTHNO ORKAE

7 OOCANERM

6 RAHBAIN

ARCTIC OCEAN

EUROPE

C

J

ASIA

D

K

A

F

AFRICA

L

A

B

INDIAN
OCEAN

PACIFIC
OCEAN

E

ANTARCTICA

13–24 MATCH EACH
COUNTRY WITH THE
CORRECT AREA AND
LETTER ON THE MAP.

GAME SHOW

ULTIMATE GEOGRAPHY CHALLENGE

1 The Uros people travel across which lake on boats made from totora reeds?

a. Lake Titicaca, Peru/Bolivia
b. Great Bear Lake, Canada
c. Lake Baikal, Russia
d. Lake Victoria, Tanzania, Kenya, and Uganda

2 TRUE OR FALSE?

The busiest road in Gibraltar cuts directly across its airport's runway.

3 Which national park in the U.S.A. receives the most visitors each year?

a. Great Smoky Mountains in Tennessee–North Carolina
b. Yosemite in California
c. Grand Canyon in Arizona
d. Acadia in Maine

4 Which three colors, sometimes called Pan-African colors, can be found on the flags of Ethiopia, Mali, and Ghana?

a. red, white, and blue
b. green, white, and purple
c. red, yellow, and green
d. pink, orange, and black

5 What percentage of the water flowing from the Niagara River goes over Horseshoe Falls?

a. none
b. 10 percent
c. 50 percent
d. 90 percent

6 Which Asian city is known as the "Venice of the East" because of its canal system?

a. Kathmandu, Nepal
b. New Delhi, India
c. Tokyo, Japan
d. Bangkok, Thailand

7 The skyline of which metropolis features more skyscrapers than New York City's?

a. Madrid
b. Hong Kong
c. Cape Town
d. Rio de Janeiro

Around the GLOBE

8 King Tut was once a resident of the country called the Gift of the Nile, also known as _____.
a. Jordan   c. Tunisia
b. Ethiopia   d. Egypt

9 Africa's Lake Malawi has more _____ than any other lake in the world.
a. tropical fish
b. freshwater sharks
c. poisonous snakes
d. water bugs

11 Which is the capital of the country known as the Emerald of the Equator?
a. Helsinki   c. Jakarta
b. Santiago   d. Harare

10 TRUE OR FALSE?
The flag of China features a Thunder Dragon with jewels in its claws.

12 On which continent would you be most likely to eat *caakiri*, a couscous pudding containing raisins, cream, and nutmeg?
a. South America   c. Europe
b. Africa   d. Australia

13 It is illegal to import what to Libya?
a. kites   c. pork
b. radios   d. candy

14 TRUE OR FALSE?
People get around Havana, Cuba, in egg-shaped vehicles called Coco Taxis.

15 ULTIMATE BRAIN BUSTER
COMPETITORS IN THE YUKON ARCTIC ULTRA CAN RACE 300 MILES (482.8 KM) IN EXTREME COLD BY ANY METHOD EXCEPT WHAT?
a. sled dog
b. on foot
c. cross-country skiing
d. mountain bike

MANY PEOPLE THINK THAT LIGHTNING MCQUEEN FROM THE CARS MOVIES WAS NAMED AFTER THE ACTOR STEVE MCQUEEN, WHO STARRED IN SEVERAL CAR-RACING MOVIES. LIGHTNING MCQUEEN ACTUALLY GETS HIS NAME FROM GLENN MCQUEEN, WHO WAS A TOP ANIMATOR AT PIXAR.

Pop CULTURE

FROM THE MOVIE CARS

On the JOB

SHERLOCK HOLMES

1 The detectives of _____ are no match for Sherlock Holmes.
- **a.** Fiji Intelligence Services
- **b.** FBI
- **c.** Scotland Yard
- **d.** Bundespollize

2 Which job might SpongeBob apply for?
- **a.** receptionist
- **b.** astronaut
- **c.** fisherman
- **d.** fry cook

3 Which industry does Homer Simpson work in?
- **a.** construction
- **b.** nuclear energy
- **c.** medicine
- **d.** baseball

SUPERMAN (CLARK KENT)

4 Clark Kent and Lois Lane are reporters for which newspaper?
- **a.** the *Daily Planet*
- **b.** the *Washington Post*
- **c.** *Gotham Gazette*
- **d.** the *New York Times*

HOMER SIMPSON

5 When he isn't hunting for ancient relics, Indiana Jones can be found in a classroom teaching what subject?
- **a.** archaeology
- **b.** world history
- **c.** jazz
- **d.** algebra

6 Edna Mode—designer of the Incredibles' costumes—refused to include which of the following accessories in her designs?
- **a.** capes
- **b.** masks
- **c.** belts
- **d.** gloves

7 Before becoming a Jedi, Luke Skywalker was a _____.

a. scientist
b. robot repairman
c. farmer
d. teacher

MARY POPPINS

8 Which superhero is also an inventor?

a. Green Lantern   c. Iron Man
b. Thor   d. Wonder Woman

9 Mary Poppins is a nanny for which family?

a. The Banks family
b. The von Trapp family
c. The Brown family
d. The Baudelaire family

10 Which museum job does Larry Daley from *Night at the Museum* have?

a. curator   c. exhibit designer
b. security guard   d. shop manager

11 Throughout the Harry Potter series, Severus Snape held all of the following job titles except _____.

a. Professor of Potions
b. headmaster of Hogwarts
c. Quidditch coach
d. Professor of Defence Against the Dark Arts

SEVERUS SNAPE

12 What job does Peter Parker do for the *Daily Bugle* newspaper?

a. reporter   c. editor
b. photographer   d. paper boy

13 In *Bee Movie*, Barry achieves his dream by becoming a _____.

a. honey stirrer   c. pollen jock
b. helmet tester   d. lawyer

14 Which muppet character is a pianist?

a. Rowlf the Dog   c. Fozzie Bear
b. Miss Piggy   d. Beaker

PAGE-TURNERS

1 What does Charlie Bucket find to enter Willy Wonka's chocolate factory?

a. a Willy Wonka chocolate bar
b. a golden ticket
c. the Great Glass Elevator
d. Oompa-Loompas

2 What character does Alice play croquet with in *Alice's Adventures in Wonderland*?

a. Cheshire Cat
b. Mad Hatter
c. White Rabbit
d. Queen of Hearts

3 Why does Meg Murry go on a journey in *A Wrinkle in Time*?

a. to rescue her father
b. to get away from her classmates
c. to find food for her family
d. to escape Aunt Beast

4 Which author wrote about her American frontier childhood in *Little House on the Prairie*?

a. Laura Ingalls Wilder
b. Emily Dickinson
c. Louisa May Alcott
d. Florence Nightingale

5 Author R. L. Stine is known for writing which popular series of books?

a. Diary of a Wimpy Kid
b. The Hunger Games
c. Goosebumps
d. Harry Potter

6 What will the winner of The 39 Clues series receive?

a. a trip around the world
b. a book of spells
c. one million dollars
d. a secret to make them the most powerful person on Earth

7 In *The Curious Incident of the Dog in the Night-Time,* **what is the family name of the boy Christopher?**

a. Davidson
b. Holmes
c. Boone
d. Stevenson

8 **True or false? The Tuck family of** *Tuck Everlasting* **remains young by eating leaves from a special tree.**

9 **Pinocchio is transformed into a real boy by _____.**

a. a fairy
b. Geppetto
c. Jiminy Cricket
d. the Fox and the Cat

10 **Fern Arable is a human character in which classic novel?**

a. *The Secret Garden*
b. *Little House in the Big Woods*
c. *Little Women*
d. *Charlotte's Web*

11 **Who is Ramona Quimby's sister?**

a. Picky
b. Susan
c. Beezus
d. Dorothy

12 **True or false? In Lemony Snicket's** *The Bad Beginning,* **Count Olaf pretends to be related to the Baudelaire children.**

13 **Percy Jackson is the son of which Greek god?**

a. Zeus
b. Hades
c. Poseidon
d. Dionysus

14 **Which character from** *The Wind and the Willows* **escapes from prison?**

a. Mole
b. Mr. Badger
c. Rat, or Ratty
d. Mr. Toad

TRUE or FALSE?
Heroes and Villains

1 OVER THE COURSE OF THE STAR WARS SERIES, LUKE SKYWALKER BECOMES THE VILLAIN, DARTH VADER.

2 SNOW WHITE FALLS INTO A DEEP SLEEP AFTER SHE PRICKS HER FINGER ON THE SPINDLE OF A SPINNING WHEEL.

3 ONE OF BAMBI'S GREATEST ENEMIES IS HUMANS.

4 KING PIG IS A TOUGH TARGET FOR THE *ANGRY BIRDS*.

5 COUNT DRACULA LIVES IN A CASTLE IN PENNSYLVANIA, U.S.A.

6 MARIO AND LUIGI THINK FAWFUL IS JUST AWFUL.

7 MISS HANNIGAN TRIES TO HELP ANNIE BY FINDING HER PARENTS.

8 THE GRINCH TRIES TO RUIN CHRISTMAS IN WHOVILLE BY STEALING THE HOLIDAY GIFTS AND DECORATIONS.

9 IN GREEK MYTHOLOGY, MEDUSA TURNS PEOPLE INTO STONE.

10 BILBO BAGGINS MUST RECLAIM A KINGDOM FROM GOLLUM IN *THE HOBBIT: AN UNEXPECTED JOURNEY*.

11 IN *PIRATES OF THE CARIBBEAN: ON STRANGER TIDES*, CAPTAIN JACK SPARROW MUST FACE BLACKBEARD.

12 IN *THE LEGEND OF ZELDA*, LINK'S ARCHNEMESIS IS THE DARK LORD GANONDORF.

13 CAPTAIN COOK SEEKS REVENGE ON PETER PAN FOR FEEDING HIS HAND TO A CROCODILE.

14 VOLDEMORT IS OFTEN REFERRED TO AS A DEATH EATER IN THE HARRY POTTER SERIES.

15 THE BIG BAD WOLF IS THE MAIN VILLAIN IN BOTH "LITTLE RED RIDING HOOD" AND "THE THREE LITTLE PIGS."

16 THE LAND OF OZ IS TERRORIZED BY THE WHITE WITCH.

17 X-MEN RIVALS PROFESSOR XAVIER AND MAGNETO STARTED OUT AS FRIENDS.

18 AFTER MR. HYDE TAKES A POTION, HE BECOMES THE EVIL DR. JEKYLL.

19 IN THE SUPERMAN SERIES, LEX LUTHOR TRIES TO DESTROY SUPERMAN BY EXPOSING HIM TO HIS WEAKNESS: IRONITE.

20 CRUELLA DE VIL KIDNAPS DALMATIAN PUPPIES BECAUSE SHE HATES THE SOUND OF THEIR BARKING.

21 IN *CARS 2*, PROFESSOR Z IS A CORVETTE.

22 PERCY GOES ON A QUEST TO FIND THE GOLDEN FLEECE IN *PERCY JACKSON: SEA OF MONSTERS*.

23 IN *RIO 2*, NIGEL SEEKS REVENGE AGAINST BLU FOR AN INJURY THAT MAKES HIM UNABLE TO FLY.

24 IN THE SONIC THE HEDGEHOG VIDEO GAME SERIES, SONIC MUST STOP DOCTOR EGGMAN FROM CONQUERING THE WORLD.

25 SHERE KHAN, A TIGER IN *THE JUNGLE BOOK*, WANTS TO EAT A YOUNG BOY NAMED MOWGLI.

26 IN *DESPICABLE ME 2*, GRU IS RECRUITED TO FIND A STOLEN TNT-LOADED SHARK ROCKET.

27 CINDERELLA'S EVIL STEPSISTERS TRY TO PREVENT HER FROM ATTENDING THE BALL BY TEARING HER MOTHER'S DRESS APART.

28 STUART LITTLE MUST PROTECT HIMSELF FROM THE FAMILY DOG AFTER HE IS ADOPTED BY THE LITTLE FAMILY.

29 IN *MATILDA*, BY ROALD DAHL, SCHOOLGIRL MATILDA OFTEN PLAYS TRICKS ON MISS HONEY.

30 THE VILLAIN ELECTRO, FROM *THE AMAZING SPIDER-MAN 2*, DEVELOPS HIS POWERS AFTER HE FALLS INTO A TANK OF ELECTRIC EELS.

CHECK YOUR ANSWERS ON PAGES 161–162.

You Can DANCE!

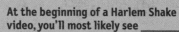

DANCING 1920s FLAPPER

1 What fast-paced 1920s dance is named after a city in South Carolina, U.S.A.?
a. Columbia
b. Sumter
c. Charleston
d. Newbury

2 True or false?
Aviator Charles Lindbergh was the first person to dance the Lindy Hop in the 1920s.

3 Which of the following is not a break-dance move?
a. jackhammer
b. worm
c. toe stand
d. windmill

BREAK DANCING

4 At the beginning of a Harlem Shake video, you'll most likely see _____ .
a. one person dancing
b. a group of people wearing masks
c. kids doing jumping jacks
d. someone singing

5 What dance move is featured in Psy's music video for "Gangnam Style"?
a. the invisible horse
b. the annoying fly
c. the angry alligator
d. the downward dog

6 In 2011, the "Party Rock Anthem" had everybody _____ .
a. moonwalking
b. tap dancing
c. shuffling
d. twisting

7 Which of the following styles is not a ballroom dance?

a. samba   c. cha-cha
b. foxtrot   d. ballet

8 True or false?
The Cabbage Patch Kids dolls of the 1980s inspired the name of a dance.

CABBAGE PATCH KIDS DOLL

9 What country is famous for inventing the modern-day tango?

a. Spain   c. Argentina
b. Italy   d. Ireland

10 What prop do you need to do the limbo?

a. a grass skirt
b. a long stick
c. sneakers
d. a tennis racket

11 In which U.S. state are you most likely to find people dancing the hula?

a. Alaska   c. Florida
b. New York   d. Hawaii

HULA DANCER

12 You put your left foot in, you put your left foot out to do the _____.

a. Hokey Pokey
b. Chicken Dance
c. Watusi
d. Running Man

13 In the 1970s, people did which of the following dances to disco music?

a. robot   c. hustle
b. twist   d. tap

14 You are most likely to see people doing a line dance to which song?

a. "Electric Boogie"   c. "Firework"
b. "The Story of My Life"   d. "Happy Birthday"

CHECK YOUR ANSWERS ON PAGES 161–162.

MAD FOR THE MOVIES

1 In the How to Train Your Dragon series, what type of dragon is Toothless?

a. Scauldron
b. Night Fury
c. Timberjack
d. Komodo

2 Which song from the movie *Frozen* won an Academy Award for best original song?

a. "Let It Go"
b. "Under the Sea"
c. "Colors of the Wind"
d. "A Whole New World"

3 True or false? After E.T. is stranded on Earth, he uses a game called *Operation* to phone home.

4 Which country is the muppet chef in *Muppets Most Wanted* from?

a. China
b. Argentina
c. Sweden
d. Cameroon

5 Which movie robot was a trash collector?

a. Wall-E
b. Optimus Prime
c. Rodney Copperbottom
d. The Iron Giant

6 How is Scar related to Simba in *The Lion King*?

a. father   c. teacher
b. friend   d. uncle

7 The line "I'll get you my pretty—and your little dog, too!" comes from which movie?

a. *Bolt*   c. *Frankenweenie*
b. *The Wizard of Oz*   d. *Beverly Hills Chihuahua*

8 True or False? Aladdin is the name of the genie in the magic lamp.

9 Who turns out to be Buzz Lightyear's father in *Toy Story 2*?

a. Buddy
b. Ken
c. Evil Emperor Zurg
d. Mr. Potato Head

10 What ancient Egyptian ruler did Mr. Peabody and Sherman meet in their 2014 movie?

a. Nefrititi
b. Ramses
c. Cleopatra
d. King Tut

11 In *Madagascar*, which animal did not escape from New York City's Central Park Zoo?
a. giraffe
b. cheetah
c. zebra
d. hippopotamus

12 In *Cars 2*, cars that have trouble running are called _____.
a. blueberries c. bananas
b. oranges   d. lemons

13 What team does Blade Ranger oversee in *Planes: Fire & Rescue*?
a. The Smokejumpers
b. The Firecrackers
c. The Flame Busters
d. The Miami Heat

14 Which princess has the longest hair?
a. Fiona
b. Rapunzel
c. Snow White
d. Mulan

GAME SHOW ULTIMATE POP CULTURE CHALLENGE

1 Which series of books was not written by Lemony Snicket?
a. All the Wrong Questions
b. Divergent Universe
c. A Series of Unfortunate Events
d. 13 Words

2 Which Disney princess kissed a frog?
a. Ariel   c. Tiana
b. Rapunzel   d. Jasmine

3 Which job might science fiction hero Dr. Who apply for?
a. auto mechanic
b. chronometer repairer
c. robot designer
d. architect

5 Ghosts were villains in what classic video game?
a. *Pitfall!*
b. *Space Invaders*
c. *Frogger*
d. *Pac-Man*

4 Which actress is the voice of Margo in the Despicable Me movies?
a. Miranda Cosgrove
b. Ariana Grande
c. Kaley Cuoco
d. Debby Ryan

6 TRUE OR FALSE?
The conga line dance was once banned in Cuba.

7

Who is the oldest Smurf?
a. Smurfette c. Papa Smurf
b. Brainy   d. Jokey

8 Actor Chris Evans has played which two famous movie heroes?

a. Captain Kirk and Iron Man
b. Thor and Indiana Jones
c. Captain America and Human Torch
d. Bilbo Baggins and Green Lantern

9 Which of these book characters is usually hard to find in a crowd?

a. Amelia Bedelia
b. Waldo
c. Curious George
d. Captain Underpants

10 Which of the following is not a 1960s dance craze that was named after a food?

a. the Frozen Yogurt
b. the Peppermint Twist
c. the Mashed Potato
d. the Dipsey Doodle

11 Which television cartoon has also been turned into a big-screen movie?

a. *Phineas and Ferb*
b. *SpongeBob SquarePants*
c. *Gravity Falls*
d. *Adventure Time*

12 What is Flat Stanley's real name?

a. Stanley Price
b. Stanley Sheepdog
c. Stanley Styles
d. Stanley Lambchop

13 What character is a villain on *Ben 10: Omniverse*?

a. Ben Tennyson
b. Rook Blonko
c. Four Arms
d. Khyber the Huntsman

14 ULTIMATE BRAIN BUSTER — Which of these figures matches its LEGO movie character name?

a.
Wyldstyle

b.
Emmet

c.
Batman

d.
Lord Business

Back to NATURE

JAPANESE MACAQUES BATHE IN HOT SPRINGS.

WHAT A GEM

1 What's the birthstone for a person **born** in April?

a. diamond
b. emerald
c. ruby
d. marble

2 The Hope Diamond is known for both its deep blue hue and **size**, which is about the same as a _____ .

a. pea
b. walnut
c. baseball
d. basketball

3 What does the word "**carat**" refer to?

a. a purple root vegetable
b. the weight of a gemstone
c. the value of gold
d. the shape of a pearl

4 In which story can you read about the **Emerald City**?

a. *Harry Potter and the Sorcerer's Stone*
b. *The Chronicles of Narnia*
c. *The Hunger Games*
d. *The Wonderful Wizard of Oz*

5 In the past, some people believed that eating ground-up **opals** could _____ .

a. make it rain
b. prevent nightmares
c. protect against lightning
d. make you live forever

6 Which sea creature **makes** pearls?

a. octopus
b. swordfish
c. oyster
d. hermit crab

7 True or false? All sapphires are blue.

8 Which summer birthstone has been found in meteorites?

a. garnet
b. amethyst
c. peridot
d. pearl

10 True or false? A diamond is so hard that it can **scratch** any other rock.

12 According to myth, which gemstone darkens in the presence of **evil**?

a. diamond
b. turquoise
c. ruby
d. sapphire

QUARTZ CRYSTAL

9 The name "garnet" came from the stone's resemblance to the **seeds** of which fruit?

a. lemon
b. pomegranate
c. watermelon
d. plum

11 What **color** is lapis lazuli?

a. blue
b. purple
c. yellow
d. green

13 Where have people **not** mined for the blue-green gemstone turquoise?

a. Egypt
b. Italy
c. Iran
d. Antarctica

14 True or false? Jade was worth more than gold in Ancient **China**.

15 What color is **topaz**, the birthstone for November?

a. yellow
b. pink
c. colorless
d. any of the above

Nature's GREATEST HITS

1 If you head to the Arctic Circle in winter, you might see colored bands in the sky at night called _____.

a. an aurora　　　**c.** color soup
b. laser lights　　　**d.** a U.F.O.

2 True or false?
There's a volcano in Indonesia that erupts sulfur gas, which burns with blue flames.

3 Yellowstone National Park has about _____ active geysers, which regularly shoot hot water and steam into the air.

a. 5　　　　　　**c.** 500
b. 50　　　　　**d.** 1,000

GEYSER

4 Where can you go to see many large, natural rock arches?

a. Paris, France　　　**c.** Utah, U.S.A.
b. São Paulo, Brazil　**d.** Hawaii, U.S.A.

5 What is a shooting star?

a. a star falling toward Earth
b. a spaceship landing
c. a star exploding
d. space dust burning up

6 Which tiny creatures make the ocean glow with blue light at night?

a. sand fleas
b. bioluminescent algae
c. mosquitoes
d. glowworms

SHOOTING STARS

7 What formed the Grand Canyon?
a. a river
b. dynamite
c. an earthquake
d. asteroid strike

8 True or false?
It's impossible to see a rainbow at night.

9 When a comet passes by Earth, you may see _____ .
a. an explosion
b. a meteor shower
c. acid rain
d. fireworks

HIKING IN THE GRAND CANYON

10 What natural spectacle often happens during a volcanic eruption?
a. tornadoes
b. lightning
c. rainbows
d. shooting stars

11 A haboob is a type of intense _____ .
a. dust storm
b. thunderstorm
c. lightning shower
d. tornado

ANGEL FALLS

12 Which color is not in a rainbow?
a. red
b. violet
c. green
d. brown

13 On which continent is Angel Falls, the tallest waterfall on Earth, where water plummets 35,376 feet (10,783 m) from top to bottom?
a. South America
b. Africa
c. Europe
d. Australia

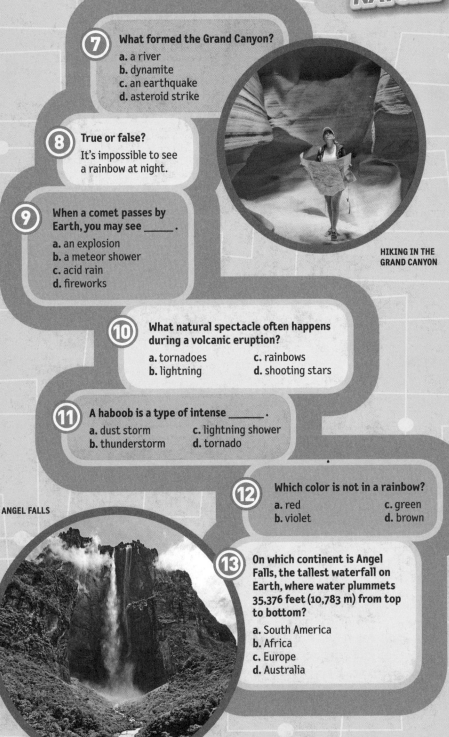

IN BLOOM

2 **Which country was the first to hold parties to celebrate when cherry trees bloom?**

a. Japan
b. India
c. Russia
d. England

1 **In 1637, a single bulb of which flower cost as much as a house in Holland?**

a. daisy
b. marigold
c. sunflower
d. tulip

3 **True or false? Bamboo stalks never produce flowers.**

4 **Which flower was a symbol of rebirth to ancient Egyptians?**

a. apple blossom
b. daffodil
c. lotus
d. bluebell

5 **Which flower is safe for people to eat?**

a. orange daylily
b. pink clover
c. violet
d. all of the above

6 **What color carnation is the national flower of Spain?**

a. white
b. red
c. pink
d. blue

7 **True or false? A sunflower can grow taller than an ostrich.**

FIELD OF TULIPS

8 What is the most popular **flower** to give your sweetheart on Valentine's Day?

a. lily
b. rose
c. foxglove
d. dandelion

9 Which country grows over half of the cut flowers sold in the United States?

a. Italy
b. Turkey
c. Canada
d. Colombia

10 There are orchids whose flowers look like every animal except _____.

a. elephants
b. monkeys
c. parrots
d. tigers

11 Which flower name was one of 2013's top ten most popular names for **baby girls?**

a. Violet
b. Poppy
c. Lily
d. Jasmine

12 What forms in the **center** of a white daisy?

a. red pollen
b. large black seeds
c. many tiny yellow flowers
d. a juicy strawberry

13 Which common flower is poisonous to humans, horses, and **many** other animals?

a. dandelion
b. clover
c. rhododendron
d. honeysuckle

14 True or false? There is a flower that smells like **chocolate.**

CHECK YOUR ANSWERS ON PAGES 163–164.

MAP MANIA!
FANTASTIC FORESTS

Diverse forests cover large areas of Earth. Discover a few different types of forests here.

NORTH AMERICA

B

ATLANTIC OCEAN

PACIFIC OCEAN

F
SOUTH AMERICA

ANTARCTICA

1 REDWOOD FOREST

What color are the needles of the rare albino redwood tree?

a. black   c. white
b. blue   d. pink

2 AMAZON RAIN FOREST

More than 3,000 species of fruit grow in the Amazon rain forest, including which of the following?

a. lemon   c. mango
b. banana   d. all of the above

3 SCHWARZWALD

What does the name *schwarzwald* mean?

a. sleepy town
b. black forest
c. grasshopper
d. jungle of doom

ARCTIC OCEAN

EUROPE

A
D

A S I A

E

C

AFRICA

PACIFIC
OCEAN

INDIAN
OCEAN

AUSTRALIA

4  SUNDARBANS

Which endangered animal could
you find swimming in the waters
of Sundarbans mangrove forest?

a. Bengal tiger
b. giant panda
c. mountain gorilla
d. black rhino

5 CROOKED
FOREST

About 400 pine trees grow with
a curved base in the middle of
a forest in Poland. How did this
happen?

a. A tornado hit.
b. A giant beast stomped on them.
c. The trees have mutant DNA.
d. It's a mystery.

6 SAGANO
FOREST

In this forest in Japan,
bamboo grows at a rate of
_____ per day.

a. 1 inch (2.5 cm)
b. 12 inches (30 cm)
c. 40 inches (100 cm)
d. 60 inches (150 cm)

7–12 MATCH EACH FOREST
OR JUNGLE TO ITS
LOCATION ON THE MAP.

CHECK YOUR ANSWERS ON PAGES 163–164.

Life's a BEACH

1 Where do seagulls live?
a. ocean beaches
b. lakes
c. garbage dumps
d. all of the above

2 True or false?
Beach sand is made entirely of ground-up seashells.

3 What makes the sand in a sandcastle stick together?
a. gravity
b. water
c. seaweed
d. sunlight

SANDCASTLE

4 What is the best way to prevent sunburn?
a. bury your body in the sand
b. use sunscreen
c. get a tan
d. go swimming

5 Most shark attacks in the world occur on the beaches of _____ .
a. Florida, U.S.A.
b. South Africa
c. Brazil
d. California, U.S.A.

GREAT WHITE SHARK

6 Which animal found near the seashore has blue blood?
a. seagull
b. razor clam
c. horseshoe crab
d. sand flea

SEAGULL

7 True or false?
Every ocean beach around the world has high and low tides.

8 New Zealand is home to a beach with which unusual feature?
a. boiling hot water
b. black sand
c. ice all year long
d. a population of scorpions

9 What is a sand dollar?
a. plant
b. rock formation
c. animal
d. alien visitor

SAND DOLLAR

10 Which sea creature left behind this seashell?
a. scallop
b. oyster
c. octopus
d. whelk

11 How many arms do most starfish have?
a. 2   **c.** 13
b. 5   **d.** 100

12 What is flotsam and jetsam that you find on a beach?
a. empty seashells
b. dead seaweed
c. skeletons of dead fish
d. pieces of wrecked ships and their cargo

EXPLORING THE BEACH

CHECK YOUR ANSWERS ON PAGES 163–164.

TRUE or FALSE?
Save the Planet

1 A SHOWER ALWAYS USES UP LESS WATER THAN A BATH.

2 POPULATIONS OF MOST PLANT AND ANIMAL SPECIES ON EARTH ARE SMALL AND FEW IN NUMBER.

3 THE WORLD'S OCEANS HAVE BEEN GETTING COLDER.

4 THE POPULATION OF ENDANGERED ONE-HORNED RHINOCEROSES IS GROWING.

5 EARTH'S TOTAL POPULATION REACHED ABOUT 10 BILLION IN THE YEAR 2000.

6 AN ELEPHANT NEEDS ITS TUSKS TO SURVIVE.

7 EARTH DAY IS ON APRIL 22.

8 AN ENVIROLOGIST IS SOMEONE WHO CARES ABOUT PROTECTING THE ENVIRONMENT.

9 ON AVERAGE, A PERSON IN THE UNITED STATES THROWS AWAY 4 POUNDS (1.8 KG) OF WASTE EACH DAY.

10 THE ENDANGERED SIBERIAN TIGER ONLY LIVES IN INDIA.

11 THE MOST POLLUTED CITY IN THE WORLD IS IN EUROPE.

12 ON AVERAGE, A TELEVISION USES UP MORE ENERGY IN ONE YEAR THAN A REFRIGERATOR.

13 THE PLACE WHERE AN ANIMAL LIVES IS CALLED ITS HABITAT.

14 A POACHER IS SOMEONE WHO REFUSES TO RECYCLE.

15 DOING DISHES BY HAND USES MORE WATER THAN RUNNING A FULL DISHWASHER.

16 ON AVERAGE, ONE PLANT OR ANIMAL SPECIES GOES EXTINCT EVERY MINUTE.

17 FISH REGULARLY SWALLOW PLASTIC WASTE.

18 ACTOR LEONARDO DICAPRIO LIVES IN A SOLAR-POWERED HOUSE.

19 IN PORTLAND, OREGON, U.S.A., IT'S AGAINST THE LAW TO SERVE FOOD IN STYROFOAM CONTAINERS.

20 GLOBAL WARMING DOESN'T HAVE ANY EFFECT ON CORAL REEFS.

21 A PLASTIC MILK JUG TAKES A MILLION YEARS TO DECOMPOSE.

22 ON AVERAGE, PEOPLE IN INDIA USE MORE WATER THAN PEOPLE IN THE UNITED STATES.

23 IN 1960, LESS THAN 10 PERCENT OF ALL WASTE GOT RECYCLED.

24 YOUR TV STILL USES ELECTRICITY EVEN WHEN IT'S TURNED OFF.

25 THERE ARE NO ENDANGERED FISH SPECIES.

26 ALL PARROTS SOLD AS PETS WERE CAUGHT IN THE WILD.

27 DISPOSABLE PLASTIC WATER BOTTLES WASTE ENERGY.

28 AMPHIBIANS—FROGS, TOADS, NEWTS, SALAMANDERS, AND CAECILIANS—ARE THE MOST ENDANGERED GROUP OF ANIMALS IN THE WORLD.

29 IN 2012, PEOPLE USED MORE PLASTIC THAN PAPER.

30 HUMPBACK WHALE POPULATIONS ARE SHRINKING.

CHECK YOUR ANSWERS ON PAGES 163–164.

THE SPA TREATMENT

1 What heats up the water in a natural hot spring?
- a. the sun
- b. magma beneath the ground
- c. microscopic creatures
- d. steam engines

2 Blue Lagoon spa in Iceland formed accidentally when engineers were building a _____ .
- a. football field
- b. battleship
- c. medieval castle
- d. power plant

3 True or false?
The water of Iceland's Blue Lagoon is crystal clear below the milky blue surface.

4 True or false?
The water of Chena Hot Springs, a tourist destination in Alaska, is boiling hot.

5 If you can see steamy vapor above a hot spring, which fact must be true?
- a. The water is hotter than the air.
- b. It's summertime.
- c. The hot spring is poisonous.
- d. It's about to rain.

6 Science has shown that bathing in Blue Lagoon can _____ .
- a. treat baldness
- b. cure blindness
- c. soothe skin problems
- d. make warts disappear

7 Snow monkeys love to bathe in the hot springs in which country?
- a. Canada
- b. Italy
- c. Kenya
- d. Japan

BLUE LAGOON (MINERAL BATHS),
NEAR KEFLAVIK, ICELAND

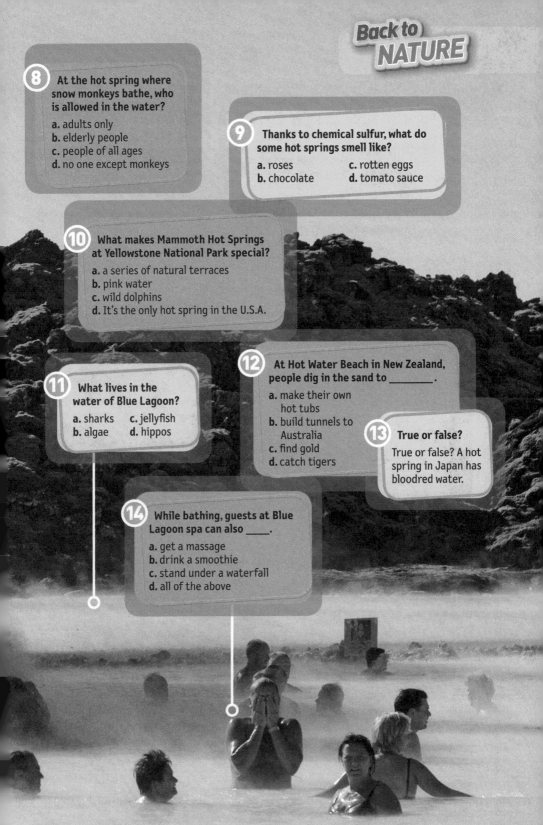

8 At the hot spring where snow monkeys bathe, who is allowed in the water?

a. adults only
b. elderly people
c. people of all ages
d. no one except monkeys

9 Thanks to chemical sulfur, what do some hot springs smell like?

a. roses
b. chocolate
c. rotten eggs
d. tomato sauce

10 What makes Mammoth Hot Springs at Yellowstone National Park special?

a. a series of natural terraces
b. pink water
c. wild dolphins
d. It's the only hot spring in the U.S.A.

11 What lives in the water of Blue Lagoon?

a. sharks
b. algae
c. jellyfish
d. hippos

12 At Hot Water Beach in New Zealand, people dig in the sand to _____.

a. make their own hot tubs
b. build tunnels to Australia
c. find gold
d. catch tigers

13 True or false?

True or false? A hot spring in Japan has bloodred water.

14 While bathing, guests at Blue Lagoon spa can also _____.

a. get a massage
b. drink a smoothie
c. stand under a waterfall
d. all of the above

GAME SHOW
ULTIMATE NATURE CHALLENGE

1 What do you call an animal or plant species that no longer exists?
a. predator   c. extinct
b. ghost   d. doodad

2 What percentage of all the water on Earth can people use for drinking?
a. less than 1 percent
b. about 10 percent
c. about 30 percent
d. more than 50 percent

3 TRUE OR FALSE?
In Hawaii, U.S.A., it's illegal to own a pet snake.

4 What can be found at the top of Mount Everest, the tallest mountain peak in the world?
a. polar bears
b. fossils of sea creatures
c. pine trees
d. a floating castle

5 Which gemstone is most often polished to a round shape?
a. diamond   c. ruby
b. sapphire   d. opal

7 A male tarantula lives for 5 to 7 years. What is a female's life span?
a. 1 year   c. about 10 years
b. 5 to 7 years d. up to 25 years

6 TRUE OR FALSE?
Many of the colors in a rainbow are invisible to human eyes.

8 What was the name of the Roman spa town in Britain now known as Bath?
a. Aquamarine
b. Aqua Vitae
c. Aquae Sulis
d. Aquarium

9 Which of these flowers is common in many forests?

a.
sunflower

c.
bluebell

b.
rose

d.
daisy

10 # TRUE OR FALSE?
All lightning bolts strike something on the ground.

11 Which type of tree was growing on Earth 350 million years ago?
a. tree fern   c. conifer
b. ash   d. maple

12 What is the state flower of Arizona, U.S.A.?
a. bluebell
b. thistle
c. Saguaro cactus flower
d. Venus flytrap

13 Not all volcanoes erupt with fiery lava. Some spew _____.
a. mud   c. orange juice
b. snow   d. glitter

15 ULTIMATE BRAIN BUSTER
You may find this egg case next time you visit the beach. What is it called?
a. mermaid's purse
b. shark party hat
c. sea jewel
d. ninja star

14 # TRUE OR FALSE?
There are more stars in the universe than grains of sand from all the world's beaches and deserts.

CAMEL TREK AT THE PYRAMIDS AT GIZA, EGYPT

Follow the LEADER

1 Why did France's Louis XIV, who ruled from 1638 to 1718, wear a wig and high heels?
a. as signs of royalty
b. they were in fashion
c. to look tall
d. to show off his long legs

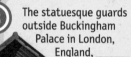

LOUIS **XIV**

2 **True or false?** There are countries that have both a president and a prime minister.

3 The statuesque guards outside Buckingham Palace in London, England, _____ .
a. keep their lunch under their hats
b. are actors
c. are trained soldiers
d. blow whistles to call police officers

4 Which Egyptian pharaoh known as "the boy king" began his rule at the age of nine?
a. Khufu
b. Tutankhamun
c. Zeus
d. Ramses II

5 Egypt's last pharaoh made the country one of the strongest powers in the world. Who was she?
a. Seti
b. Thutmose
c. Delilah
d. Cleopatra

6 Which of the following is named for Julius Caesar, ancient Rome's ruler from 49 B.C. to 44 B.C.?
a. the Caesar salad
b. the month of July
c. the drink "Orange Julius"
d. all the above

PETER THE GREAT

7 Peter the Great was tsar of Russia in the 1600s. Who added "the Great" to his name?
a. Attila the Hun
b. his wife
c. his mother
d. he did

BUCKINGHAM PALACE GUARD

8 **True or false?** Ming, Qing, Song, Tang, Xin, and Ping are all names of ancient Chinese dynasties.

9 In Europe during medieval times, what could only royalty wear?
a. underwear
b. hats
c. purple or gold silk fabric
d. jewelry

10 How many countries currently have kings and queens?
a. 1 to 5
b. 6 to 10
c. 11 to 20
d. more than 20

11 When John F. Kennedy became president of the United States in 1961, he invited which poet to read a poem during the inauguration ceremony?
a. Shel Silverstein
b. Robert Frost
c. Kenn Nesbitt
d. Roald Dahl

12 Which world leader was in jail for about 27 years before he was elected president?
a. Bill Clinton
b. Mahatma Gandhi
c. Nelson Mandela
d. Vladimir Putin

JOHN F. KENNEDY

13 From 1206 to 1227, which fierce leader established the Mongol Empire, which later became the world's largest empire under a single border?
a. Ivan the Terrible
b. Genghis Khan
c. Akbar the Great
d. Bubba the Wise

14 **True or false?** Greenland has its own prime minister, yet it belongs to Denmark.

CHECK YOUR ANSWERS ON PAGES 164–165.

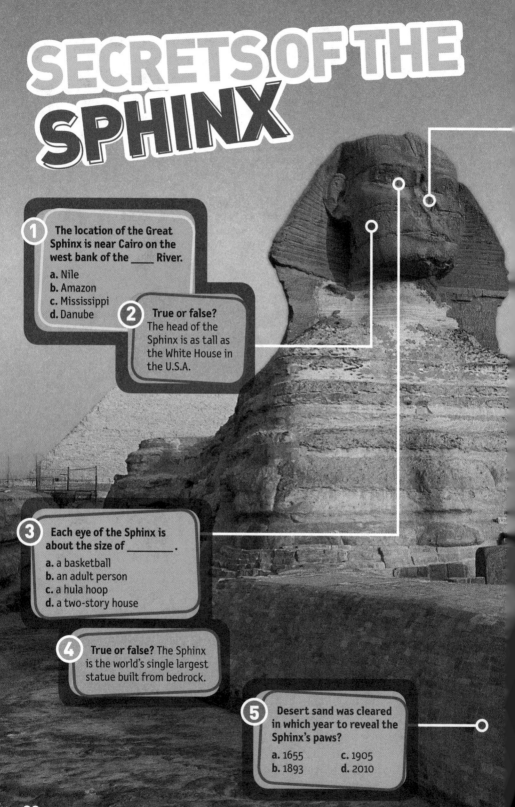

SECRETS OF THE SPHINX

1 The location of the Great Sphinx is near Cairo on the west bank of the _____ River.

a. Nile
b. Amazon
c. Mississippi
d. Danube

2 True or false? The head of the Sphinx is as tall as the White House in the U.S.A.

3 Each eye of the Sphinx is about the size of _____.

a. a basketball
b. an adult person
c. a hula hoop
d. a two-story house

4 True or false? The Sphinx is the world's single largest statue built from bedrock.

5 Desert sand was cleared in which year to reveal the Sphinx's paws?

a. 1655
b. 1893
c. 1905
d. 2010

6 What do historians think happened to the Sphinx's nose?

a. Desert winds blew it away.
b. An angry camel bit it off.
c. It was blown off during soldiers' target practice.
d. No one knows for sure.

7 Today we can see the entire statue, but for hundreds of years the Sphinx was buried up to its _____.

a. chin   c. temples
b. chest   d. shoulders

8 Further excavation of the Sphinx revealed _____.

a. a baby sphinx by the left paw
b. a curled tail by the right paw
c. a tablet saying "Made for Rameses II" on the front
d. a temple of the Sun God behind it

9 Erosion due to weather has changed the Sphinx over the years. What feature did it have originally but no longer possesses?

a. sideburns   c. a necklace
b. a braided beard d. arms

10 True or false? The Great Sphinx is the only ancient sphinx statue ever unearthed in Egypt.

11 The Sphinx dates to about 2500 B.C. When first built, it _____.

a. was painted in bright colors
b. had windows to an inner chamber
c. had no head
d. was two separate statues

12 The Sphinx is in the Sahara. The word "sahara" is Arabic for _____.

a. sand
b. mighty
c. desert
d. windy

13 True or false? The remains of a large community were uncovered near the Sphinx. That's where the workers who built the Sphinx lived.

CHECK YOUR ANSWERS ON PAGES 164–165.

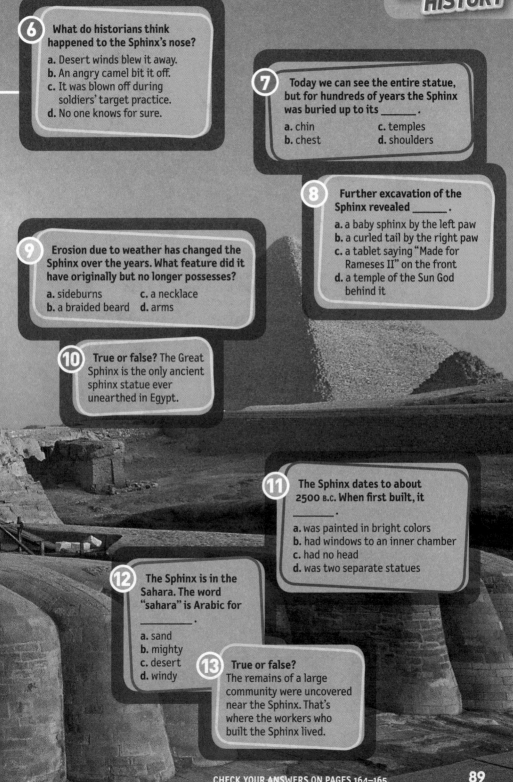

Cool CRITTERS

LAIKA

1 In 1957, a dog from Russia named Laika made history. It was the first animal _____.
a. to speak to humans
b. to survive a heart transplant
c. to travel to space
d. to watch *Star Trek*

2 Cher Ami (meaning "dear friend" in French) transported messages between French and American troops during World War I. Which type of animal was she?
a. a racing greyhound
b. a carrier pigeon
c. a hawk
d. a horse

3 Scientist Jane Goodall watched chimps make tools and learn sign language. What did she conclude from her observations?
a. The chimps were one of a kind.
b. They liked human friends.
c. Chimps may be smarter than people thought.
d. They had been in the jungle too long.

CHIMPANZEE

4 In 1925, Balto, a sled dog, journeyed 1,000 miles (1,609 km) for medicine that saved thousands of lives. In his honor, Alaska has _____.
a. the Iditarod Dog Sled Race
b. free vaccines for everyone
c. named a highway along Balto's route for him
d. a sled-dog parade

5 The discovery of fossils of *Archaeopteryx*, a dinosaur with feathers and wings, shows how dinosaurs are related to _____.
a. planes
b. bats
c. birds
d. flying squirrels

ARCHAEOPTERYX

6 In 1974, scientists found the skeleton of a three-million-year-old female ape that walked on two legs. Why did they name her Lucy?

a. A Beatles' song with that name was on the radio.
b. She looked like Lucy from *Peanuts*.
c. Lucy means "lucky lady."
d. Lucy is a popular woman's name.

7 Saint Bernard is a breed of working dog from Italy and Switzerland. It's trained to rescue people who are _____ .

a. stuck in tunnels and subways
b. buried in deep snow
c. trapped in fires
d. lost in parks

8 In addition to pigeons, armies have used elephants, camels, horses, and dogs in war. Sergeant Stubby was the U.S. Army's first war dog. Which war did he fight in?

a. The French and Indian War
b. The American Civil War
c. World War I
d. World War II

9 **True or false?** Charles Darwin developed his theory of evolution and natural selection by studying a variety of finches on the Galápagos Islands.

SAINT BERNARD

10 Stories tell of Ancient Egyptian pharaoh Cleopatra dying by snakebite. However, she really died from _____ .

a. a monkey bite
b. drinking poison
c. her own sword
d. indigestion

EGYPTIAN COBRA

11 **True or false?** The Tower of London in England keeps ravens on its grounds in the belief that they protect the castle and the royal family.

TOWER OF LONDON

CHECK YOUR ANSWERS ON PAGES 164–165.

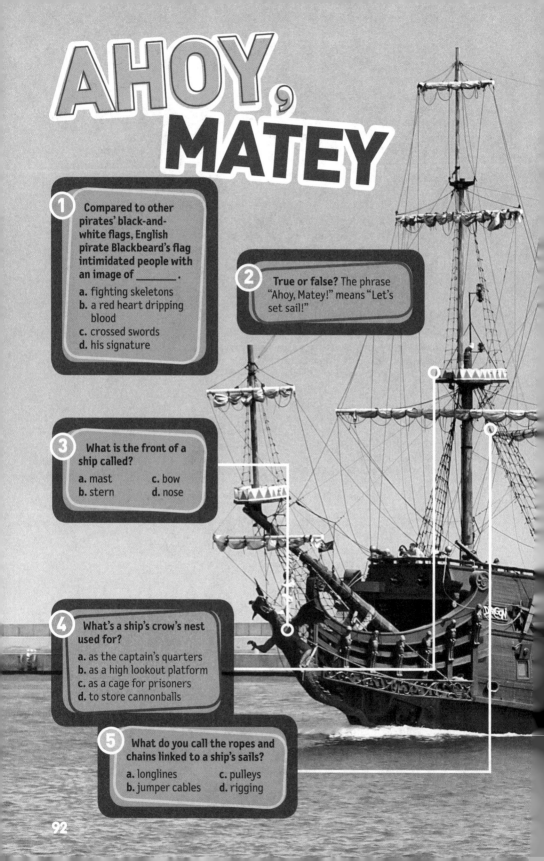

AHOY, MATEY

1 Compared to other pirates' black-and-white flags, English pirate Blackbeard's flag intimidated people with an image of _____.

a. fighting skeletons
b. a red heart dripping blood
c. crossed swords
d. his signature

2 **True or false?** The phrase "Ahoy, Matey!" means "Let's set sail!"

3 What is the front of a ship called?

a. mast
b. stern
c. bow
d. nose

4 What's a ship's crow's nest used for?

a. as the captain's quarters
b. as a high lookout platform
c. as a cage for prisoners
d. to store cannonballs

5 What do you call the ropes and chains linked to a ship's sails?

a. longlines
b. jumper cables
c. pulleys
d. rigging

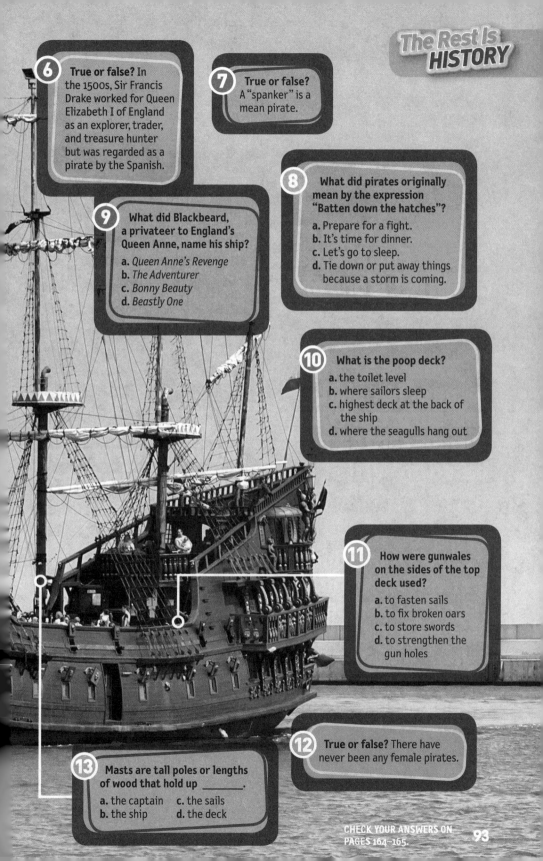

6 **True or false?** In the 1500s, Sir Francis Drake worked for Queen Elizabeth I of England as an explorer, trader, and treasure hunter but was regarded as a pirate by the Spanish.

7 **True or false?** A "spanker" is a mean pirate.

8 What did pirates originally mean by the expression "Batten down the hatches"?
a. Prepare for a fight.
b. It's time for dinner.
c. Let's go to sleep.
d. Tie down or put away things because a storm is coming.

9 What did Blackbeard, a privateer to England's Queen Anne, name his ship?
a. *Queen Anne's Revenge*
b. *The Adventurer*
c. *Bonny Beauty*
d. *Beastly One*

10 What is the poop deck?
a. the toilet level
b. where sailors sleep
c. highest deck at the back of the ship
d. where the seagulls hang out

11 How were gunwales on the sides of the top deck used?
a. to fasten sails
b. to fix broken oars
c. to store swords
d. to strengthen the gun holes

12 **True or false?** There have never been any female pirates.

13 Masts are tall poles or lengths of wood that hold up _____.
a. the captain   c. the sails
b. the ship   d. the deck

CHECK YOUR ANSWERS ON PAGES 164–165.

GAME NIGHT

1 True or false? The Ancient Egyptian game of **senet** is one of the oldest board games.

2 This red-and-black board game is seen worldwide. It's called "draughts" in England. What's the game called in the U.S.A.?

a. Uno
b. checkers
c. Clue
d. Parcheesi

3 Whist is a card game of fun, skill, and surprise. What serious card game is based on **whist**?

a. go fish
b. bridge
c. solitaire
d. war

4 In which country did the game of mah-jongg **originate**?

a. India
b. Turkey
c. Greece
d. China

5 In Norway, this game's name means "twiddles and bears" and in **England** it is called "noughts and crosses." In the U.S.A., this game is _____.

a. tic-tac-toe
b. labyrinth
c. Connect Four
d. Scrabble

6 Chutes and Ladders is similar to snakes and ladders, which was played in **India** in the 1500s to teach _____.

a. counting
b. cheating
c. memory enhancement
d. the difference between good deeds and bad deeds

7 In what part of the world is the game mancala very popular?

a. Asia
b. Africa
c. South America
d. Australia

8 In France, this single-deck card game is sometimes called "success," in Britain it's "patience," and in the U.S.A. it's ____.

a. Life
b. Boggle
c. solitaire
d. gin rummy

9 In the seventh century, players equated playing ____ with skill and **genius!** What's this game?

a. Candy Land   c. Tiddlywinks
b. Risk   d. chess

10 The ancient Royal Game of ur is a race for two players using dice and **pawns**. It is similar to today's ____.

a. backgammon   c. scoop
b. checkers   d. red light, green light

11 What board game came out during the Great Depression of the **1930s** in the U.S.A. when jobs and money were scarce?

a. Sorry!   c. Monopoly
b. Life   d. Apples to Apples

12 Which game, like checkers and **chess**, is practically the same as it was in ancient times?

a. Parcheesi   c. Candy Land
b. Risk   d. Clue

13 **True or false?** The game we know today as jacks was originally played with animal bones and pebbles.

TRUE or FALSE?
They Did What?

1. IN 1492, COLUMBUS SET SAIL TO PROVE THE WORLD WAS NOT FLAT.

2. U.S. SECRETARY OF STATE WILLIAM H. SEWARD PURCHASED FLORIDA FROM SPAIN FOR MORE THAN $7 MILLION, WHICH WAS CONSIDERED A BAD INVESTMENT.

3. IN 1967, A SMALL VILLAGE IN ECUADOR ELECTED A FOOT POWDER FOR MAYOR.

4. IN 1626, NATIVE AMERICANS ACCEPTED ABOUT $24 IN EXCHANGE FOR LAND THAT WAS LATER TO BECOME PART OF NEW YORK CITY.

5. IN THE EARLY 1800S, DOCTORS NEVER WASHED THEIR HANDS OR INSTRUMENTS, SO ABOUT HALF OF ALL SURGERIES RESULTED IN DEATH DUE TO INFECTION.

6. IN 1999, A $125 MILLION MARS ORBITER LOST ITS WAY IN SPACE BECAUSE NASA'S SPACE TEAM USED INCORRECT MEASUREMENTS.

7. *TITANIC*, DESIGNED AS AN "UNSINKABLE SHIP," SUNK ON ITS FIRST VOYAGE IN 1912. THE CREW IGNORED WARNINGS OF ICEBERGS IN THEIR PATH.

8. FRANCE'S NAPOLEON BONAPARTE TRIED TO INVADE RUSSIA WITH A MASSIVE ARMY IN 1812. MOST OF THE ARMY LEFT BECAUSE THEY HAD NOT BEEN PAID.

9. DECCA RECORDS TURNED DOWN AN AUDITION BY 1960S GROUP THE BEATLES, BUT THE COMPANY DID SIGN ONE DIRECTION MANY YEARS LATER.

10. TWELVE PUBLISHERS REJECTED J. K. ROWLING'S *HARRY POTTER AND THE SORCERER'S STONE* BEFORE BLOOMSBURY ACCEPTED IT.

11. IN ABOUT 1180 B.C., TROY BROUGHT INSIDE ITS WALLED CITY A GIANT WOODEN HORSE FILLED WITH EGYPTIAN SOLDIERS, WHO THEN KILLED THE TROJANS.

12. THE GERMAN AIRSHIP *HINDENBURG* WAS KEPT AFLOAT BY BEING FILLED WITH OXYGEN, A HIGHLY FLAMMABLE GAS.

13. ALEXANDER THE GREAT, LEADER OF THE PERSIAN EMPIRE IN ABOUT 340 B.C., DIED AT AGE 32. BY THEN HE HAD CONQUERED MUCH OF AFRICA AND EUROPE.

14. IN 1928, SCIENTIST ALEXANDER FLEMING DISCOVERED THE ANTIBIOTIC PENICILLIN BY ACCIDENT WHEN TIDYING UP AFTER AN EXPERIMENT.

15. DURING WORLD WAR II, SCIENTIST JAMES WRIGHT INVENTED AN ARTIFICIAL RUBBER THAT WASN'T VERY RUBBERY, BUT IT WAS LATER USED TO MAKE SILLY PUTTY.

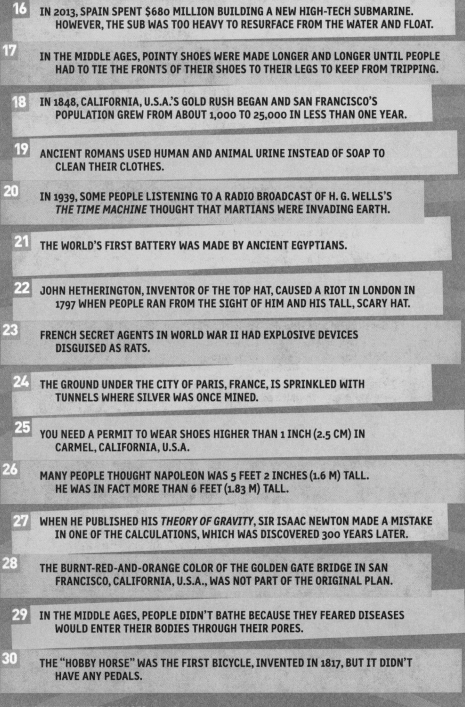

16 IN 2013, SPAIN SPENT $680 MILLION BUILDING A NEW HIGH-TECH SUBMARINE. HOWEVER, THE SUB WAS TOO HEAVY TO RESURFACE FROM THE WATER AND FLOAT.

17 IN THE MIDDLE AGES, POINTY SHOES WERE MADE LONGER AND LONGER UNTIL PEOPLE HAD TO TIE THE FRONTS OF THEIR SHOES TO THEIR LEGS TO KEEP FROM TRIPPING.

18 IN 1848, CALIFORNIA, U.S.A.'S GOLD RUSH BEGAN AND SAN FRANCISCO'S POPULATION GREW FROM ABOUT 1,000 TO 25,000 IN LESS THAN ONE YEAR.

19 ANCIENT ROMANS USED HUMAN AND ANIMAL URINE INSTEAD OF SOAP TO CLEAN THEIR CLOTHES.

20 IN 1939, SOME PEOPLE LISTENING TO A RADIO BROADCAST OF H. G. WELLS'S *THE TIME MACHINE* THOUGHT THAT MARTIANS WERE INVADING EARTH.

21 THE WORLD'S FIRST BATTERY WAS MADE BY ANCIENT EGYPTIANS.

22 JOHN HETHERINGTON, INVENTOR OF THE TOP HAT, CAUSED A RIOT IN LONDON IN 1797 WHEN PEOPLE RAN FROM THE SIGHT OF HIM AND HIS TALL, SCARY HAT.

23 FRENCH SECRET AGENTS IN WORLD WAR II HAD EXPLOSIVE DEVICES DISGUISED AS RATS.

24 THE GROUND UNDER THE CITY OF PARIS, FRANCE, IS SPRINKLED WITH TUNNELS WHERE SILVER WAS ONCE MINED.

25 YOU NEED A PERMIT TO WEAR SHOES HIGHER THAN 1 INCH (2.5 CM) IN CARMEL, CALIFORNIA, U.S.A.

26 MANY PEOPLE THOUGHT NAPOLEON WAS 5 FEET 2 INCHES (1.6 M) TALL. HE WAS IN FACT MORE THAN 6 FEET (1.83 M) TALL.

27 WHEN HE PUBLISHED HIS *THEORY OF GRAVITY*, SIR ISAAC NEWTON MADE A MISTAKE IN ONE OF THE CALCULATIONS, WHICH WAS DISCOVERED 300 YEARS LATER.

28 THE BURNT-RED-AND-ORANGE COLOR OF THE GOLDEN GATE BRIDGE IN SAN FRANCISCO, CALIFORNIA, U.S.A., WAS NOT PART OF THE ORIGINAL PLAN.

29 IN THE MIDDLE AGES, PEOPLE DIDN'T BATHE BECAUSE THEY FEARED DISEASES WOULD ENTER THEIR BODIES THROUGH THEIR PORES.

30 THE "HOBBY HORSE" WAS THE FIRST BICYCLE, INVENTED IN 1817, BUT IT DIDN'T HAVE ANY PEDALS.

CHECK YOUR ANSWERS ON PAGES 164–165.

Keep Your HAT ON!

COWBOY HAT

1 **True or false?** In ancient Greece, former slaves wore small felt hats to show they were free men.

2 **What do cowboys' broad-brimmed, high-crowned hats do for them?**
a. made them look handsome
b. protected them from sun and rain
c. hid their faces
d. made them look mysterious

3 **Which men's hat associated with film star Humphrey Bogart was first a popular woman's hat after actress Sarah Bernhardt wore it on stage in 1882?**
a. the beret
b. the top hat
c. the fedora
d. the turban

4 **In which country are shady, cone-shaped straw hats, popularly known as "rice paddy hats," worn?**
a. China
b. Cambodia
c. Japan
d. all of these

5 **Which brimless, red, cone-shaped hat with a black tassel was once the Turkish national headdress?**
a. fez
b. captain's hat
c. turban
d. beehive

6 **True or false?** Only Native American male chiefs or warriors wore ceremonial feather headdresses.

7 U.S. president Abraham Lincoln stood 6 feet 4 inches (1.93 m) and was fond of wearing which 7- to 8-inch (17.8- to 20.3-cm)-high hat?
a. a Stetson   c. a stovepipe
b. a bowler   d. a fedora

8 The origin of the party hat is unknown. But hats with a pointed shape are traditionally a symbol of _____ .
a. candle-blowing skills   c. power
b. luck   d. wisdom

PARTY HAT

9 Which hat was made popular by 1930s actors Charlie Chaplin and Laurel and Hardy?
a. beret
b. bonnet
c. bowler
d. pillbox

10 True or false? The cloche, which is French for "bell," was a fitted hat popular with women in the 1920s.

CLOCHE HAT

11 What type of hat did detective Sherlock Holmes wear?
a. homburg
b. straw Panama hat
c. deerstalker
d. peaked cap

12 Duchess of Cambridge Kate Middleton started a fashion for small decorative hats called _____ .
a. agitators
b. fascinators
c. negotiators
d. facilitators

AGAINST THE ODDS

1 Robert Peary and Matthew Henson of the U.S. Navy reached the North Pole in _____.

a. 1996
b. 1750
c. 1909
d. 1850

2 Jesse Owens, the grandson of slaves, won four **Olympic** gold medals in 1936. His world record for the long jump lasted for _____.

a. 4 years
b. 25 years
c. 50 years
d. has never been broken

3 True or false? Helen Keller was both blind and deaf but still earned a college degree and became a writer and teacher.

4 Jim Abbott had a winning sports career despite being born without a right hand. What **sport** did Jim play?

a. soccer
b. ice hockey
c. football
d. baseball

5 True or false? Amelia Earhart was the first woman to fly **solo** around the world.

6 About how many people joined Martin Luther King, Jr., on his 1963 March on Washington for equal rights for **African** Americans?

a. 10,000　　c. 100,000
b. 50,000　　d. 200,000

7 In 1927, Charles Lindbergh made a solo flight between New York and Paris, earning him which **nickname**?

a. Champion Chuck　　c. The Flying Eagle
b. Lucky Lindy　　　　d. Fast Flyer

8 Susan B. Anthony, the first woman to have her face on a circulating U.S. coin, fought for _____ .

a. peace　　　　　c. women's rights
b. animal rights　d. clean air

"NEAREST THE POLE," COMMANDER ROBERT E. PEARY PLANTING THE AMERICAN FLAG.

9 Mahatma Ghandi used nonviolent protests to lead India to freedom from which country's rule?

a. Great Britain　c. Russia
b. United States　d. China

10 As a child, Wilma Rudolph had **polio** and had difficulty walking, yet she became _____ .

a. a runner who earned three Olympic gold medals
b. a photographer
c. a movie star
d. a writer

MAP MANIA!
PERFECT PALACES

Here's your chance to take a royal tour of some of the world's greatest palaces.

① ALHAMBRA CASTLE

This castle was created by which group that lived in Spain for 200 years until about 1442?

a. the Greeks
b. the Moors
c. the Cherokee
d. the Romans

② THE FORBIDDEN CITY

In Beijing, China, this giant palace was home to 24 emperors for nearly 500 years. What structure surrounds and protects that palace?

a. heavy arches and doors
b. armed guards
c. a deep, wide moat of water
d. guard dogs

③ BUCKINGHAM PALACE

Only two people are responsible for winding the 350 _____ in England's royal palace.

a. windmills
b. music boxes
c. clocks
d. window blinds

4 NEUSCHWANSTEIN CASTLE

This German castle was built for Ludwig II of Bavaria and was the inspiration for _____.

a. Donald Trump's house
b. Sleeping Beauty Castle in Disneyland
c. a new reality show
d. Prince William and Kate Middleton's home

EUROPE
ASIA
D
E
AFRICA
PACIFIC OCEAN
INDIAN OCEAN
AUSTRALIA

5 KREMLIN

In Russian, the word *kremlin* means fortress and the one in Moscow is the largest in the world. The Kremlin contains _____.

a. the country's schools
b. a museum and a library
c. a sports arena
d. five palaces and four cathedrals

6 PALACE OF VERSAILLES

France's Louis XVI and his wife Marie-Antoinette lived here. Louis spent one-third of the Versailles budget just on water because he loved _____.

a. fountains
b. boat races
c. swimming
d. baths

7–12 MATCH EACH PALACE TO ITS CORRECT LOCATION ON THE MAP.

CHECK YOUR ANSWERS ON PAGES 164–165.

GAME SHOW

ULTIMATE HISTORY CHALLENGE

① TRUE OR FALSE?
The Great Pyramid of Giza is so large that astronauts can see it from space.

② An enormous statue is being built in South Dakota, U.S.A. Construction started in 1948, but it is not yet complete. What Lakota war hero does it honor?
a. Geronimo
b. Tecumseh
c. Crazy Horse
d. Cochise

③ What is the protective hat worn by soldiers called?
a. a crown   c. a helmet
b. a busby   d. a shell cap

④ What do people call the more than 1,000-year-old palace in Axum, Ethiopia?
a. Samson's Palace
b. The Queen of Sheba's Palace
c. Robin Hood's Palace
d. Emperor-With-No-Clothes Palace

⑤ TRUE OR FALSE?
Teams of U.S. Navy researchers are training pigeons to save lives at sea.

⑥ Which famous composer wrote his best works while totally deaf?
a. Mozart
b. Beethoven
c. Bach
d. Elton John

⑦ According to a pirate, what is "Davey Jones's locker"?
a. the bottom of the sea
b. a ship's toilet
c. a treasure chest
d. a captain's quarters

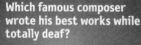

8 Britain's Queen Elizabeth II is usually seen wearing a hat. That's why a replica of her head is kept by her _____ .

a. chauffeur   c. milliner
b. doctor   d. all of these

9 TRUE OR FALSE?

At a time when few women were educated, Marie Curie became one of the few people ever to receive a Nobel Prize for both Medicine and Physics.

10 *Time* magazine found ten things that all great leaders do. Which is one of them?

a. punish wrongdoing
b. fire silly people
c. convey authority and warmth
d. ask for help when hit by a crisis

11 What childhood game, a big craze in the 1890s, involves flicking playing pieces into a pot?

a. jacks
b. jump rope rhyming
c. tiddlywinks
d. stoop ball

12 TRUE OR FALSE?

There is a sphinx in Greek mythology—a monster in Thebes who kills those who cannot solve its riddle.

13 When a pirate says, "Shiver me timbers," the pirate is expressing _____ .

a. surprise and concern
b. fear of being cold
c. a response to something funny
d. a dare

15 ULTIMATE BRAIN BUSTER

Thomas Edison was fired from his job and nearly penniless when he invented the _____ in 1877.

a.

telephone

c.

microphone

b.

television

d.

phonograph

14 Topkapi, located in Istanbul, Turkey, is the oldest and largest intact palace in the world. In 1924, it was turned into _____ .

a. a hotel   c. a spa for sultans
b. a movie set   d. a museum

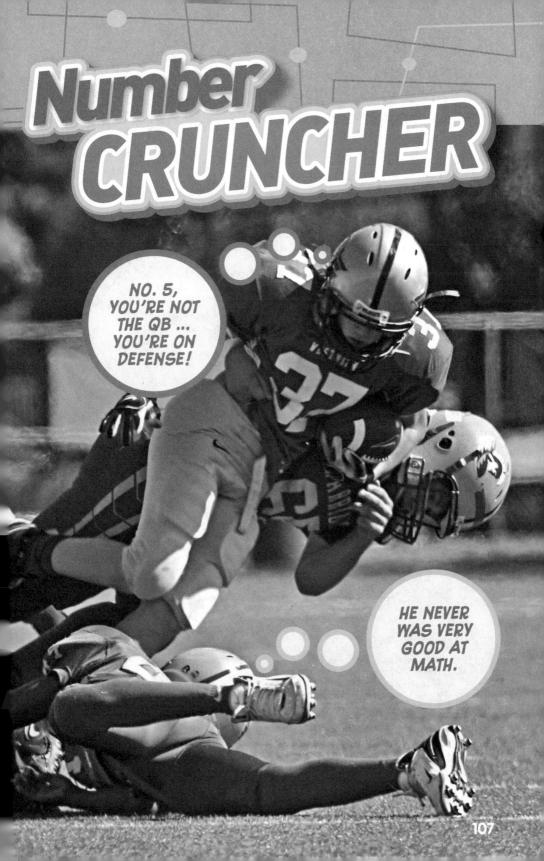

At the BALLGAME

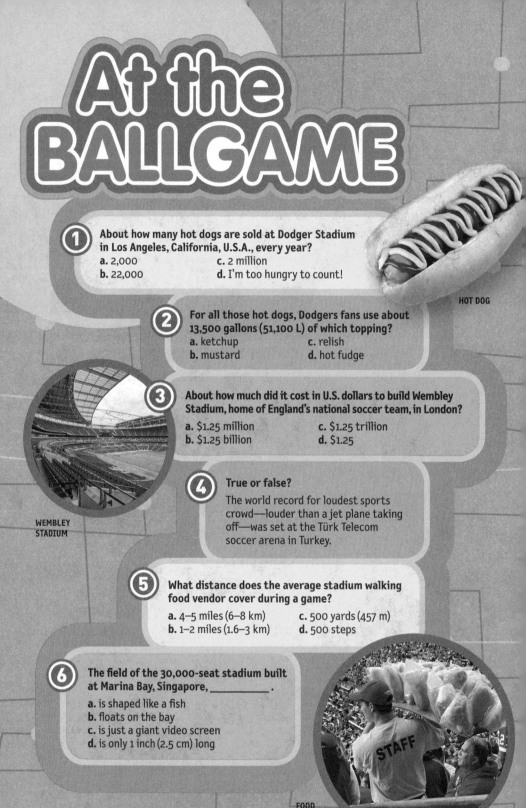

1. About how many hot dogs are sold at Dodger Stadium in Los Angeles, California, U.S.A., every year?
   - **a.** 2,000
   - **b.** 22,000
   - **c.** 2 million
   - **d.** I'm too hungry to count!

HOT DOG

2. For all those hot dogs, Dodgers fans use about 13,500 gallons (51,100 L) of which topping?
   - **a.** ketchup
   - **b.** mustard
   - **c.** relish
   - **d.** hot fudge

3. About how much did it cost in U.S. dollars to build Wembley Stadium, home of England's national soccer team, in London?
   - **a.** $1.25 million
   - **b.** $1.25 billion
   - **c.** $1.25 trillion
   - **d.** $1.25

WEMBLEY STADIUM

4. True or false?
   The world record for loudest sports crowd—louder than a jet plane taking off—was set at the Türk Telecom soccer arena in Turkey.

5. What distance does the average stadium walking food vendor cover during a game?
   - **a.** 4–5 miles (6–8 km)
   - **b.** 1–2 miles (1.6–3 km)
   - **c.** 500 yards (457 m)
   - **d.** 500 steps

6. The field of the 30,000-seat stadium built at Marina Bay, Singapore, _____ .
   - **a.** is shaped like a fish
   - **b.** floats on the bay
   - **c.** is just a giant video screen
   - **d.** is only 1 inch (2.5 cm) long

STAFF

FOOD VENDOR

BASEBALL BATTER

7 True or false?

The Ericsson Globe, home to Sweden's ice hockey team, is modeled after the sun, with distant structures representing the planets in our solar system.

8 At Miller Park in Milwaukee, Wisconsin, U.S.A., what race takes place after the sixth inning of every Brewers' baseball game?

a. race between fastest player on each team
b. race between the mayor and a fan
c. race between people dressed as sausages
d. race to get to the parking lot first after a game

9 What is the tradition involving the number 8 at the Detroit Red Wings hockey arena in Michigan, U.S.A.?

a. All fans wear jersey number 8.
b. After games, the team skates in a series of figure 8s.
c. During games, fans throw an eight-legged octopus on the ice.
d. Everyone sings "Happy Birthday" to an 8-year-old.

10 In 2011, only about 350 people watched a baseball game at the 75,000-seat Sun Life Stadium in Florida, U.S.A., because _____ .

a. the game had changed cities due to a hurricane
b. it was really hot that day
c. the home team was really, really bad
d. stadium staff couldn't unlock the stadium's doors

11 True or false?

Before international games, New Zealand rugby players do a special dance called the haka.

12 In an official cricket match, what is the maximum time allowed for a drink break during hot weather?

a. 5 minutes
b. 10 minutes
c. 30 minutes
d. 60 minutes

GREAT WALL

2 Work on the Great Wall began in about 220 B.C. When was the wall completed?

a. before 100 B.C.
b. in the 1600s
c. in the 1900s
d. by the end of 2008

1 True or false? The 12,427-mile (20,000-km) Great Wall of China is actually a series of many unconnected **walls.**

3 The part of the wall built for China's first emperor, Qin Shi Huang, known as Wan Li Chang Cheng, is 10,000 *li* long. How long is one *li*?

a. 1 foot (30.5 cm)
b. 1 yard (0.9 m)
c. 1/3 mile (0.5 km)
d. as long as the emperor's foot

4 True or false? The 40-foot (12-m) towers along the wall were built to make sure Emperor Qin's people didn't escape.

5 In Qin's time, what percentage of China's total population was involved in building the Great Wall?

a. 1 percent
b. 10 percent
c. 20 percent
d. 50 percent

6 According to estimates, about how many people died while building the Great Wall for **Qin?**

a. 0
b. 400
c. 4,000
d. 400,000

7 Much of the wall—about 5,500 miles (8,932 km)—was built at a time in China's history known as _____.

a. the Ming dynasty
b. the Communist Revolution
c. Days of the Last Emperor
d. the British Invasion

8 To help protect China, there were **six fortresses** with large gates built along the wall. These are called _____.

a. golden doors
b. passes
c. stations
d. rest stops

9 What is the average height of the Great Wall of China?

a. 8 feet (2.4 m)
b. 25 feet (7.6 m)
c. 50 feet (15 m)
d. 5,280 feet (1.6 km)

10 True or false?
The Great Wall is so big it can be seen by **astronauts** on the International Space Station.

11 What is the width of the Great Wall at its narrowest point?

a. 4 inches (10.2 cm)
b. 4 yards (3.7 m)
c. 4 feet (1.2 m)
d. 4 miles (6.4 km)

12 What is the width of the Great Wall at its widest point?

a. 55 feet (16.8 m)
b. 5.5 feet (1.7 m)
c. 5 inches (12.7 cm)
d. 55 miles (88.5 km)

13 True or false?
Every year since 1999, runners have visited China to participate in the Great Wall Marathon including a route with 5,164 steps (up and down).

CHECK YOUR ANSWERS ON PAGES 166–167.

Two Can Play THAT GAME

PING-PONG PADDLES

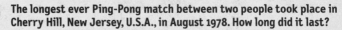

1 The longest ever Ping-Pong match between two people took place in Cherry Hill, New Jersey, U.S.A., in August 1978. How long did it last?

a. 132 minutes
b. 31 hours
c. 132 hours 31 minutes
d. It isn't finished yet.

2 True or false?
Padded boxing gloves were used first by English boxers in a match in France in 1818.

3 At the 1984 Winter Olympics, English ice dancers Torvill and Dean received a 6.0 for "artistic impression." What was special about that?

a. It was the first time all judges gave the same score.
b. It was the first time all judges gave a perfect score.
c. It was the lowest average score in Olympic history.
d. It happened at 6 p.m. on the 6th day of the month.

TORVILL AND DEAN

4 Not counting the cue ball, how many pool balls are used in a regular game of pool?

a. 8
b. 9
c. 15
d. Whoops, we lost one!

5 For Olympic synchronized swimming, what is the official temperature of the water?

a. 78.8°F (26°C)
b. 65°F (18.3°C)
c. 50.5°F (10.3°C)
d. 32°F (0°C)

POOL BALLS

6 In 1925, in which odd place did stuntpeople Gladys Roy and Ivan Unger try to play tennis?

a. between the 20- and 50-yard lines on a football field
b. 3,000 feet (0.9 km) up, on the wing of a flying biplane
c. 6,000 feet (1.8 km) down, at the bottom of the Grand Canyon
d. inside a 25-foot (7.6-m) truck driving down the highway

7 What is the name for the contest when two people run with one person's right leg tied to the other person's left leg?

a. two-person tag race
b. four-legged race
c. three-legged race
d. two-leg tie race

8 True or false?

In the United States, handball is a game played with seven players on a court, but in the rest of the world it is a different game between two players.

FENCER

9 In fencing, the nine different blade positions are named after the words for first, second, third, and so on, in what language?

a. French   c. English
b. Spanish   d. Pig Latin

10 In lawn bowls, the small target ball is known as the jack or _____.

a. puck   c. shuttlecock
b. kitty   d. tee

11 What command does a wrestling referee shout when he wants the timekeeper to stop or start the clock?

a. "Time change"   c. "Clock clock"
b. "Chronometer"   d. "Cluck cluck"

DARTBOARD

12 True or false?

In a common version of darts, each player begins with a score of 501 and tries to be the first to reach zero.

TRUE or FALSE?

Numbers in Nature

1 SPIDERS HAVE EIGHT LEGS.

2 ANTS HAVE EIGHT LEGS.

3 AT 379 FEET 4 INCHES (115.6 M), A PINE TREE NAMED "THE GIANT" IN CALIFORNIA, U.S.A., IS THE WORLD'S TALLEST TREE.

4 JELLYFISH HAVE BEEN AROUND FOR MORE THAN 500 MILLION YEARS—THAT'S BEFORE DINOSAURS.

5 GREENLAND'S NATIONAL PARK, THE WORLD'S LARGEST, COVERS 390,000 SQUARE MILES (1,010,095 SQ KM)—AN AREA BIGGER THAN EGYPT.

6 BIRDS' EYEBALLS TAKE UP ABOUT 50 PERCENT OF THEIR HEADS, WHILE HUMANS' EYEBALLS ARE ONLY ABOUT 5 PERCENT OF OUR HEADS.

7 ACCORDING TO THE UNITED NATIONS, EVERY DECEMBER 11 IS INTERNATIONAL MOUNTAIN DAY.

8 WILD CHIMPANZEES ARE ONLY FOUND IN TEN COUNTRIES IN AFRICA.

9 THE WORLD'S LARGEST FLOWER, INDONESIA'S *RAFFLESIA ARNOLDII*, CAN GROW TO 7 FEET (2.1 M) ACROSS.

10 ABOUT 71 PERCENT OF EARTH'S SURFACE IS COVERED BY WATER.

11 MORE THAN 95 PERCENT OF THE EARTH'S WATER IS IN THE OCEANS.

12 SNAKES SHED THEIR SKIN ONCE A DAY.

13 THE TOP SPEED OF A GARDEN SNAIL IS ONE YARD (0.9 M) AN HOUR.

14 THE MEAT-EATING BLADDERWORT PLANT CAN TRAP A SMALL INSECT IN 1/50 OF A SECOND.

15 COAL IS MADE OF PLANTS THAT DIED ABOUT 300 MILLION YEARS AGO.

16 PIGS MAKE MORE THAN 20 DIFFERENT NOISES TO COMMUNICATE WITH ONE ANOTHER.

17 THE WORLD'S LONGEST LASTING RAINBOW COULD BE SEEN ABOVE SHEFFIELD, ENGLAND, FOR SIX HOURS ON MARCH 14, 1994.

18 A MOTHER ELEPHANT IS PREGNANT FOR UP TO THREE YEARS.

19 THE WORLD'S LARGEST VOLCANO, MAUNA LOA IN HAWAII, U.S.A., TAKES UP ABOUT 2,000 SQUARE MILES (5,200 SQ KM).

20 THE RAINIEST SPOT ON EARTH IS IN JAPAN. IT GETS 467 INCHES (1,186 CM) OF RAIN PER YEAR.

21 DESERTS COVER ABOUT ONE-QUARTER OF EARTH'S SURFACE.

22 GRASSHOPPERS HAVE A TOTAL OF FIVE EYES.

23 EARTHQUAKES CAN HAPPEN IN ALL 50 OF THE UNITED STATES OF AMERICA.

24 CHEETAHS GET MORE AND MORE SPOTS AS THEY GET OLDER.

25 THE VOLTAGE PRODUCED BY AN ELECTRIC EEL IS ABOUT THE SAME AS A WALL SOCKET.

26 INUITS, OR ESKIMOS, IN CANADA HAVE MORE THAN 50 DIFFERENT WORDS TO DESCRIBE TYPES OF SNOW.

27 THE HIGHER YOU GO UP A MOUNTAIN, THE GREATER THE TEMPERATURE NEEDED TO BOIL WATER.

28 OWLS CAN TURN THEIR HEADS IN A COMPLETE 360-DEGREE CIRCLE.

29 DEER SHED THEIR ANTLERS ONCE A YEAR.

30 THE HIGHEST RECORDED WIND SPEED IN A TORNADO WAS 302 MILES AN HOUR (486 KM/H) IN 1999 IN OKLAHOMA, U.S.A.

CHECK YOUR ANSWERS ON PAGES 166–167.

NINE TO FIVE

1 Most professional dancers retire between the ages of _____.

a. 60 and 65
b. 40 and 45
c. 30 and 35
d. 20 and 25

2 About what total distance do all U.S. Postal Service mail carriers and truck drivers drive per year?

a. 120,000 miles (193,000 km)
b. 1.2 million miles (1.9 million km)
c. 1.2 billion miles (1.9 billion km)
d. 1.2 miles (1.9 km)

3 True or false? The first nursing school, started in about 250 B.C. in India, was attended only by men.

4 On average, the protective gear that a firefighter wears weighs _____.

a. 10 pounds (4.5 kg)
b. 30 pounds (13.6 kg)
c. 75 pounds (34 kg)
d. 300 pounds (136 kg)

5 Which of these jobs was held by the most people in the U.S.A. in 2013?

a. police officer
b. salesperson in a store
c. waiter/waitress
d. writer of trivia questions

6 Which of these jobs is a Maasai tribeswoman in Africa expected to do each day?

a. collect water
b. collect firewood
c. milk the family cows
d. all of the above

7 On average, how many years of education (after high school) does it take to become a **doctor** in Europe?

a. 11 to 14 years
b. 5 to 6 years
c. 2 to 3 years
d. 1 really hard year

8 True or false? The traditional number of **folds** in a chef's tall hat—100—stands for the different number of ways to prepare eggs.

9 In which place do people work the most hours per **year**?

a. Great Britain
b. Germany
c. France
d. Hong Kong

10 In 1910, Raymonde de Laroche of France became the first **woman** to earn an international license to be a _____.

a. doctor
b. pilot
c. lawyer
d. chauffeur

11 Farmers first appeared in about 10,000 B.C. in Asia. How many **different** types of crops did they grow?

a. 3
b. 8
c. 24
d. 3 billion

12 Many Japanese workers begin the day at their **jobs** with a few minutes of _____.

a. drinking a cup of "workers' tea"
b. saying hello to every coworker
c. doing exercises to music played over the radio
d. looking online for a better job

13 True or false? Soccer players in **Brazil** have earned more than $1 million a month.

MAP MANIA!

MONUMENTAL NUMBERS

Test your knowledge of scale with these supersize structures.

ARCTIC OCEAN

NORTH AMERICA

ATLANTIC OCEAN

● E

● F

SOUTH AMERICA

PACIFIC OCEAN

1 THE SHARD

At 1,016 feet (310 m), this is the tallest building in Western Europe. Why is it called "The Shard"?

a. It is named after the architect, Joseph Shard.
b. It is shaped like a shard—a long, thin, pointed piece—of glass.
c. "Shard" is the old English word meaning "great height."
d. Someone misspelled "Shark."

2 GATEWAY ARCH

How do visitors get to the top of this 630-foot (192-m) monument?

a. walk up 377 steps
b. take a high-speed elevator
c. ride in one of 16 tram cars
d. fly in a helicopter

3 EIFFEL TOWER

About how many light bulbs are there on the 1,063-foot (324-m) Eiffel Tower?

a. 20,000 bulbs
b. 5,000 bulbs
c. 500 bulbs
d. 1, at the top

4 AMAZONIA ARENA

Built for soccer's 2014 World Cup, what did designers want this 44,500-seat stadium to look like?

a. a giant spiderweb
b. a big tire
c. a colorful basket of Brazilian fruit
d. a big mouth screaming at the sky

EUROPE

C

A

D

A S I A

AFRICA

B

PACIFIC OCEAN

INDIAN OCEAN

AUSTRALIA

6 YURI GAGARIN MONUMENT

Yuri Gagarin is honored by this 131-foot (40-m) statue for being _____.

a. the first human to reach space
b. the first president of Russia
c. an Olympic track hero
d. the man who carved the statue

5 ANGKOR WAT

How wide is the moat that surrounds this gigantic Hindu temple?

a. 55 feet (16.8 m)
b. 623 feet (190 m)
c. 1,111 feet (338.6 m)
d. Our tape measure fell in the water.

7–12
MATCH EACH OF THESE MIGHTY MONUMENTS TO THE RED DOT THAT SHOWS ITS CORRECT LOCATION ON THE MAP.

CHECK YOUR ANSWERS ON PAGES 166–167.

GAME SHOW

ULTIMATE NUMBER CHALLENGE

1 ## TRUE OR FALSE?

In the U.S.A., new commercial airline pilots are required to have at least 500 hours of flight time.

2 About how many people visit the Great Wall of China each year?

a. 10
b. 10,000
c. 10 million
d. 10 billion

3 Dating back to 1908, which two-person sport is the oldest at the Winter Olympics?

a. luge (sleds)
b. pairs figure skating
c. speed skating
d. snowman building

4 Usually 70 to 90 feet (21 to 27 m) long and weighing 100 to 150 tons (90,000 to 136,000 kg), this is the largest animal on Earth.

a. blue whale
b. African elephant
c. great white shark
d. really big squirrel

5 The Washington Nationals named an 8-pound (3.6-kg) burger after star pitcher Stephen Strasburg: The StrasBurger. What did it cost?

a. $5.90   c. $59
b. $9.50   d. free with ticket

6 What mode of transportation was used to carry materials when building the famous Taj Mahal in India?

a. about 1,000 trucks
b. about 1,000 elephants
c. about 1,000 donkeys
d. about 1,000 dalmatians

7 The grass tennis courts at the All England Club in Wimbledon, England, are mowed every day to about which height?

a. 1/3 inch (8 mm)
b. 1 inch (25 mm)
c. 3 inches (7.6 cm)
d. 1 foot (30.5 cm)

8 Charles Wright of the U.S.A. taught piano and was a music teacher longer than anyone else in the world. For how many years did he teach?

a. 91 years   c. 53 years
b. 76 years   d. 2 years

9 In 2005, what did Danny Way do near a 61-foot (18.6-m) gap in the Great Wall of China?

a. painted it with purple dots
b. dressed as a "human wall" and stood there for 24 hours
c. jumped over the wall on a skateboard
d. climbed the wall with suction cups

10 ## TRUE OR FALSE?

About 90 percent of an iceberg is hidden under water.

11 The Washington Monument in Washington, D.C., was built in two phases: 1848–56 and 1876–84. Which was *not* a reason for the break?

a. lack of money
b. political troubles
c. shortage of white rocks
d. uncertainty that the U.S. government would last

12 ## TRUE OR FALSE?

To watch gladiators at the Colosseum in ancient Rome, battle spectators entered through arches numbered with Roman numerals.

13 Thumb wrestling is usually a contest held between two people. What is the world record for people in a chain thumb wrestling for five straight minutes?

a. 307 people   c. 2,311 people
b. 957 people   d. 3 people

14 ULTIMATE BRAIN BUSTER

Which of the following is the loudest land animal?

a. African elephant
b. yellow labrador
c. howler monkey
d. grizzly bear

CHECK YOUR ANSWERS ON PAGES 166–167.

Down to a SCIENCE

I THINK ONE MORE DROP SHOULD JUST ABOUT DO IT!

SCHOOL STUDENTS DOING A SCIENCE EXPERIMENT

IT'S NOT THAT I'M NERVOUS ... I JUST REMEMBER WHAT HAPPENED LAST TIME THESE TWO DID AN EXPERIMENT.

TO THE MOON

1 Which of the following can't be found on the moon?
a. dust   c. craters
b. insects   d. footprints

2 Who was the first person to walk on the moon?
a. Michael Collins
b. Neil Armstrong
c. Amelia Earhart
d. Buzz Aldrin

3 What keeps the U.S. flag standing out straight and not folded against the pole?
a. The wind is blowing.
b. A horizontal bar holds it up.
c. The low gravity is too weak to pull it down.
d. The photo was faked.

4 Which country sent the first person into outer space?
a. U.S.S.R.
b. France
c. United States
d. China

5 Early astronomers called each dark splotch on the moon's surface *mare*, which is the Latin word for _____ .
a. mother   c. black
b. mosquito   d. sea

6 When astronauts on the Apollo 11 mission to the moon returned home, where did they land?
a. in a field full of cows
b. in Florida, U.S.A.
c. in the Pacific Ocean
d. in the Sahara

7 True or false?
The rocket that launched the Apollo 15 spacecraft into space also landed on the moon.

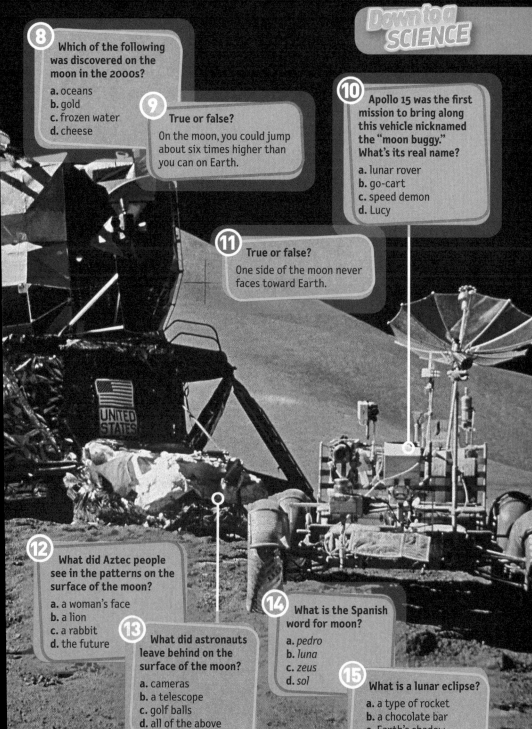

8 Which of the following was discovered on the moon in the 2000s?

a. oceans
b. gold
c. frozen water
d. cheese

9 True or false?
On the moon, you could jump about six times higher than you can on Earth.

10 Apollo 15 was the first mission to bring along this vehicle nicknamed the "moon buggy." What's its real name?

a. lunar rover
b. go-cart
c. speed demon
d. Lucy

11 True or false?
One side of the moon never faces toward Earth.

12 What did Aztec people see in the patterns on the surface of the moon?

a. a woman's face
b. a lion
c. a rabbit
d. the future

13 What did astronauts leave behind on the surface of the moon?

a. cameras
b. a telescope
c. golf balls
d. all of the above

14 What is the Spanish word for moon?

a. *pedro*
b. *luna*
c. *zeus*
d. *sol*

15 What is a lunar eclipse?

a. a type of rocket
b. a chocolate bar
c. Earth's shadow covering the moon
d. a game played on the moon

UNITED STATES

FOOD FOR THOUGHT

RICE WHEN HARVESTED

1 Rice grows in paddies, which are fields that are _____.

a. on a mountain   c. underwater
b. in a forest   d. underground

SQUARE WATERMELONS

2 Why do some farmers in Japan grow square watermelons?

a. to keep away bugs
b. They're more fun to smash.
c. They're easy to store and ship.
d. They taste better.

3 True or false?
People can safely eat cooked acorns.

4 Which country has the largest population of vegetarians?

a. India
b. United States
c. Russia
d. Japan

5 Which animal's milk is good to drink?

a. camel
b. water buffalo
c. goat
d. all of the above

6 In the 1400s, which food had never been tasted in Europe, Asia, or Africa?

a. rice   c. tea
b. chocolate   d. chicken

WATER BUFFALO

7 In the 1700s, many Europeans thought which food was poisonous?

a. apple   c. broccoli
b. tomato   d. lemon

8 Which of the following is considered a vegetable but is actually a fruit?

a. broccoli
b. spinach
c. cucumber
d. artichoke

9 About how much did the largest pumpkin ever grown weigh?

a. 100 pounds (45 kg)
b. 500 pounds (227 kg)
c. 2,000 pounds (907 kg)
d. 4,000 pounds (1,814 kg)

PUMPKIN

10 True or false?

A common red food coloring is made from crushed bugs.

11 Which food grows underground?

a. potato
b. peanut
c. carrot
d. all of the above

12 What ingredients do you need to make ice cream at home?

a. cream, sugar, ice, salt
b. chocolate, strawberries
c. milk, eggs, flour
d. baking soda, vinegar, water

BRAINBOX

1 Which animal has the **largest** brain?

a. elephant   c. shark
b. gorilla   d. sperm whale

2 A person who has bibliophobia is afraid of _____.

a. marshmallows   c. baboons
b. books   d. doctors

3 What do you call the brain cells that send and receive **signals**?

a. neurons   c. minions
b. amoebas   d. sparklers

4 True or false? Brain tissue doesn't feel any **pain**.

5 The brain disorder schizophrenia may **cause** which of the following?

a. repetitive motions
b. hallucinations
c. memory problems
d. all of the above

6 Which bird has a spongy bone around its brain to prevent **damage** when it hunts for food?

a. woodpecker
b. robin
c. eagle
d. hummingbird

7 What effect does yawning have on the **brain**?

a. reboots it   c. increases alertness
b. adds new cells   d. all of the above

8 True or false? The bigger your brain is, the smarter you are.

9 **Where do some spider brains grow?**

a. on their web
b. in a detachable sac
c. inside their legs
d. in their teeth

10 **At what age does the human brain stop growing and developing?**

a. at birth
b. age 5 to 10
c. age 11 to 16
d. after age 20

11 **What's the name for the fear of water?**

a. neptunophobia
b. hydrophobia
c. itchiphobia
d. H_2O panic

12 **Which ocean critter eats its own brain after it finds a place to attach itself and grow?**

a. clam
b. sea squirt
c. seahorse
d. squid

13 **A newborn baby's brain weighs about as much as _____ .**

a. a grape
b. a banana
c. a can of soup
d. a watermelon

14 **True or false? Humans only use 10 percent of their brainpower.**

15 **Which historical figure had the highest estimated IQ?**

a. Queen Elizabeth I
b. Leonardo da Vinci
c. George Washington
d. Charles Darwin

ON THE MOVE

1 Which part of an airplane is called the fuselage?

a. wing
b. engine
c. tail
d. body

JET PLANE

2 Which vehicle can go faster than the speed of sound?

a. motor boat
b. helicopter
c. fighter jet
d. submarine

3 Ethanol is a type of fuel that can power cars. What is it made of?

a. corn
b. sugarcane
c. grass
d. any of the above

4 How many wheels does a unicycle have?

a. 1
b. 3
c. 4
d. 10

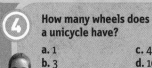

5 Which vehicle do construction crews use to create a flat surface?

a. road grader
b. excavator
c. dump truck
d. crane

6 What type of vehicle is a catamaran?

a. plane
b. boat
c. train
d. bulldozer

7 What's a common nickname for a helicopter?

a. bumblebee   c. big bird
b. chopper   d. whizzer

8 How does a submarine sink deeper into the water?

a. Jet engines drive it down.
b. Tanks fill with water to weigh it down.
c. An anchor drags it down.
d. Trained dolphins pull it.

SUBMARINE

9 Which type of brakes do most tractor-trailer trucks use?

a. air brakes   c. pedal stop
b. drum brakes   d. silly putty

10 Which of these companies makes the most expensive cars?

a. Ford   c. Volkswagen
b. Honda   d. Lamborghini

11 Which type of railroad system is used to scale mountains?

a. funicular
b. cogwheel
c. hydraulic
d. all of the above

12 If you plan to turn right in a sailboat, what should you say?

a. thatta way   c. starboard
b. blinkers on   d. righty-tighty

CHECK YOUR ANSWERS ON PAGES 167–168.

WATER WORKS

1 A WATER MOLECULE CONTAINS ONE HYDROGEN AND ONE OXYGEN ATOM.

2 THE DEPTH OF THE MARIANA TRENCH—THE DEEPEST SPOT IN THE OCEAN— IS LESS THAN THE HEIGHT OF MOUNT EVEREST.

3 A PERSON CAN SURVIVE FOR A MONTH WITH NO WATER.

4 LAKE BAIKAL IN SIBERIA IS THE DEEPEST LAKE IN THE WORLD.

5 HIPPOPOTAMUS BABIES ARE BORN UNDERWATER.

6 VOLCANIC ERUPTIONS SPEW WATER VAPOR INTO THE AIR.

7 URINE AND SPIT ARE THE ONLY TWO WAYS FOR WATER TO LEAVE THE HUMAN BODY.

8 ULTRAPURE WATER TASTES BITTER.

9 IT TAKES MORE WATER TO RAISE CHICKENS THAN TO RAISE COWS.

10 RAIN, SNOW, AND HAIL ARE ALL FORMS OF PRECIPITATION.

11 THE PLANET MERCURY CONTAINS FROZEN WATER LEFT BEHIND BY COMET STRIKES.

12 ALLIGATORS HAVE GILLS THAT ALLOW THEM TO BREATHE UNDERWATER.

13 FALLING RAIN IS TEARDROP SHAPED.

14 WATER MOLECULES FORM IN OUTER SPACE.

15 THE SAHARA IN AFRICA IS THE DRIEST PLACE ON EARTH.

16 WATER MAKES UP MORE THAN HALF OF YOUR BODY WEIGHT.

17 YOU SHOULDN'T POUR HOUSE PAINT DOWN THE DRAIN.

18 UNSAFE WATER LEADS TO MORE DEATHS WORLDWIDE EACH YEAR THAN AIR POLLUTION.

19 THE RIVER OTTER IS AN ENDANGERED SPECIES.

20 EARTH'S OCEANS CONTAIN MORE WATER THAN EVERY RIVER, LAKE, AND GLACIER COMBINED.

21 CHLORINE IS A CHEMICAL COMMONLY USED TO CLEAN POOL WATER.

22 WHEN RAIN SOAKS INTO THE GROUND, IT GETS STUCK THERE AND CAN'T MOVE.

23 ALL JELLYFISH HAVE STINGING TENTACLES.

24 NOTHING LIVES IN THE DEAD SEA.

25 THERE IS A CERTAIN TYPE OF ROCK THAT CONTAINS WATER.

26 A STARFISH HAS AN EYE AT THE END OF EACH LEG.

27 NEW YORK CITY BANNED THE SALE OF PLASTIC WATER BOTTLES IN 2013.

28 RAIN ON THE PLANET VENUS IS MADE OF SULFURIC ACID.

29 IN AFRICA, MANY WOMEN AND GIRLS WALK LONG DISTANCES EVERY DAY CARRYING HEAVY CONTAINERS OF WATER ON THEIR HEADS.

30 THE TOTAL AMOUNT OF WATER ON EARTH INCREASES EVERY YEAR.

CHECK YOUR ANSWERS ON PAGES 167–168.

MEDICAL MATTERS

1 When a person sneezes, germs can fly up to _____?

a. a few inches
b. 2 feet (0.6 m)
c. 6 feet (1.8 m)
d. 1 mile (1.6 km)

2 True or false? The appendix—part of the **digestive** system—has no useful function.

3 When did Earle Dickson invent the **Band-Aid?**

a. before the U.S. Civil War
b. at about the time U.S. women got the right to vote
c. during World War II
d. after Apollo 11 landed on the moon

4 What is the most commonly **broken** bone?

a. toe
b. nose
c. collarbone
d. finger

5 About what size is a single bacterium?

a. too small to see without a microscope
b. the size of a flea
c. the size of a grain of sand
d. larger than a grain of rice

6 What is the most common reason that **children** have to go to the doctor?

a. broken bone
b. ear infection
c. trouble sleeping
d. bee sting

7 True or false? Each person has a unique set of toeprints and fingerprints.

8 **If your snot** turns greenish and you have a fever, which ailment might be to blame?

a. chicken pox   c. sinus infection
b. pink eye   d. the plague

9 **Which technology do doctors use to see broken bones?**

a. laser scan   c. sonar
b. infrared camera   d. x-ray

10 **True or false?** More than 25 percent of **kids** have at least one food allergy.

11 **True or false?** Doctors once used blood-sucking leeches to treat diseases.

12 **Which plant can help soothe minor burns?**

a. aloe vera   c. bamboo
b. dandelion   d. poison ivy

13 **What allows the flu virus to spread more easily in the winter?**

a. hats and mittens   c. cold, dry air
b. snow fall   d. opening presents

14 **True or false?** Kids' bones **heal** faster than adults' bones.

BACTERIA SEEN THROUGH A MICROSCOPE

Can You Hear ME NOW?

CASSINI
SPACECRAFT

1 What are the two symbols that make up Morse code?
a. dots and dashes
b. beeps and blats
c. high and low whistles
d. Xs and Os

2 What system have ships used to communicate with one another for 150 years?
a. whistles
b. radar
c. signal flags
d. the Internet

3 How does the Cassini spacecraft, currently orbiting Saturn, talk to NASA engineers on Earth?
a. Antennas transmit radio waves.
b. Astronauts fly back and forth.
c. Lights flash Morse code.
d. Speakers blare really loudly.

4 What allowed England and America to communicate with each other in the late 1800s?
a. text messages
b. telegraph cable under the ocean
c. giant satellite dishes
d. smoke signals

5 About how much did it cost to buy a cell phone in 1984?
a. $19.99
b. $250
c. $4,000
d. $1 million

MOTOROLA

EARLY CELL PHONE

6 True or false?
An early experimental telephone was made using a sausage skin.

7 Which online communication company came first?
a. Twitter   c. Skype
b. Snapchat   d. Instagram

8 What system did Native Americans develop to trade with tribes that spoke different languages?
a. sign language   c. complex whistles
b. hieroglyphics   d. Pictionary

9 Which TV show featured video calls similar to Skype long before the technology was invented?
a. *SpongeBob SquarePants*
b. *Star Trek*
c. *Sesame Street*
d. *The X-Files*

SMART WATCH

10 Fax machines send messages through _____?
a. radio waves   c. laser beams
b. telephone lines d. Morse code

11 What did Alexander Graham Bell say in the first ever telephone call?
a. "Hello, world!"
b. "This isn't working."
c. "Do you have any peanuts?"
d. "Mr. Watson, come here."

12 True or false?
It's impossible to make a cell phone call while underwater.

137

MAP MANIA!
DESTINATIONS IN DANGER

These amazing places are in danger of disappearing forever due to natural changes or disasters, or human impact.

1 GREAT BARRIER REEF

What causes coral bleaching, when coral reefs turn white and die?

a. global climate change
b. high tides
c. king crabs
d. spray paint

NORTH AMERICA

ATLANTIC OCEAN

PACIFIC OCEAN

SOUTH AMERICA

B

E

2 DEAD SEA

As the Dead Sea shrinks due to its water supply being reduced, what natural disaster keeps happening along the shore?

a. hurricanes
b. hail storms
c. sinkholes
d. locust swarms

3 THE SOUTH POLE

Which South Pole animal is in great danger of disappearing due to rising temperatures?

a. giant panda
b. emperor penguin
c. polar bear
d. mosquito

4 THE EVERGLADES

Which type of tree helps protect the everglades from rising sea levels?

a. mangrove
b. pine tree
c. baobab
d. palm tree

ARCTIC OCEAN

EUROPE
C
D
A S I A

PACIFIC
OCEAN

AFRICA
A

INDIAN
OCEAN

AUSTRALIA
F

ANTARCTICA

5 CONGO BASIN

What is causing the destruction of the enormous Congo Basin rain forest?

a. mudslides
b. people are cutting down trees
c. a beetle invasion is killing trees
d. elephants are uprooting trees

6 ALPINE GLACIERS

Which phenomenon is causing glaciers in the Alps to shrink in size?

a. earthquakes
b. hurricanes
c. floods
d. global climate change

7–12 MATCH EACH DESTINATION TO ITS LOCATION ON THE WORLD MAP.

GAME SHOW
ULTIMATE SCIENCE CHALLENGE

1 Which food was worth as much as gold in the sixth century?
a. coffee   c. steak
b. bananas   d. salt

3 Which aircraft first lifted a person into the sky?
a. airplane   c. hot air balloon
b. helicopter   d. hang glider

2 TRUE OR FALSE?
A jellyfish has no brain.

4 The people of the Maldives may have to move to another country soon. What threatens these islands?
a. man-eating plants
b. rising sea levels
c. volcanoes
d. alien invasion

5 Which organ controls the balance of water in your body?
a. lungs
b. appendix
c. kidneys
d. intestines

6 What bicycle gear is most efficient when pedaling downhill?
a. high gear
b. medium gear
c. low gear
d. any of the above

7 When is flu season in Australia?
a. January and February
b. May through October
c. all year long
d. you can't catch the flu there

8 **TRUE OR FALSE?**
A dog has walked on the moon.

9 **TRUE OR FALSE?**
During the day, the surface of the moon can get hotter than the hottest temperature ever recorded in Death Valley, California, U.S.A.

10 **What did early telephone operators do with switchboards?**
a. fix broken phones
b. listen to secret conversations
c. crack codes during wartime
d. connect callers to the right line

11 **What does ··· --- ··· stand for in Morse code?**
a. Hello
b. BRB (Be right back)
c. S.O.S. (Help!)
d. LOL (Haha)

12 **Which of these is not a deadly virus?**
a. rabies   c. dengue
b. ebola   d. mumu

13 **In which city is it illegal to plant grass on your front lawn?**
a. Las Vegas, Nevada, U.S.A.
b. Paris, France
c. Cape Town, South Africa
d. Tokyo, Japan

14 **An IQ test measures how smart you are. What does "IQ" stand for?**
a. intelligence quotient
b. interbrain quiz
c. instant quickness
d. impressive quack

15 **ULTIMATE BRAIN BUSTER**
Which vegetable has "eyes" that can sprout new plants?

a.
broccoli

b.
cucumber

c.
potato

d.
green beans

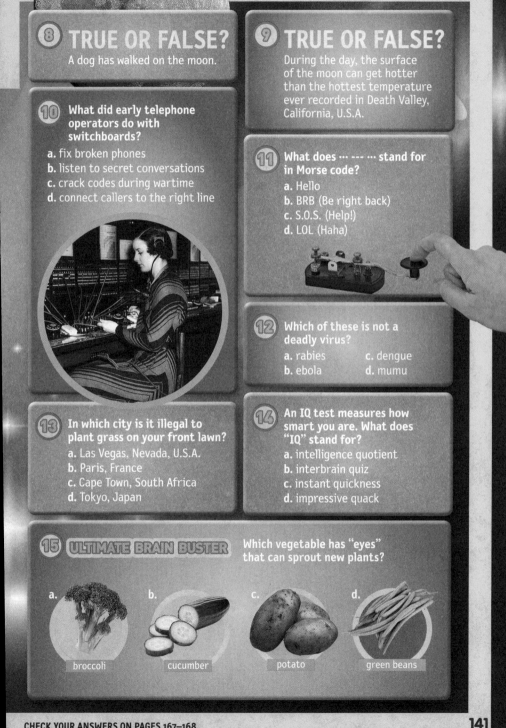

World of ADVENTURE

HE LOOKS FLIPPED OUT!

I BET THEY THINK I'VE GONE OFF THE RAILS.

SKATEBOARDER WITH FRIENDS IN A SKATEPARK

Native KNOW-HOW

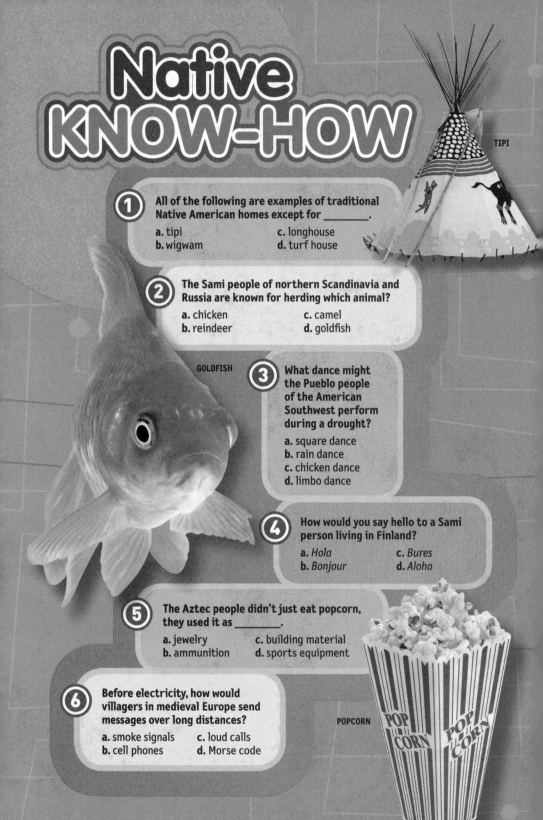

TIPI

1 All of the following are examples of traditional Native American homes except for _____.
a. tipi
b. wigwam
c. longhouse
d. turf house

2 The Sami people of northern Scandinavia and Russia are known for herding which animal?
a. chicken
b. reindeer
c. camel
d. goldfish

GOLDFISH

3 What dance might the Pueblo people of the American Southwest perform during a drought?
a. square dance
b. rain dance
c. chicken dance
d. limbo dance

4 How would you say hello to a Sami person living in Finland?
a. *Hola*
b. *Bonjour*
c. *Bures*
d. *Aloha*

5 The Aztec people didn't just eat popcorn, they used it as _____.
a. jewelry
b. ammunition
c. building material
d. sports equipment

6 Before electricity, how would villagers in medieval Europe send messages over long distances?
a. smoke signals
b. cell phones
c. loud calls
d. Morse code

POPCORN

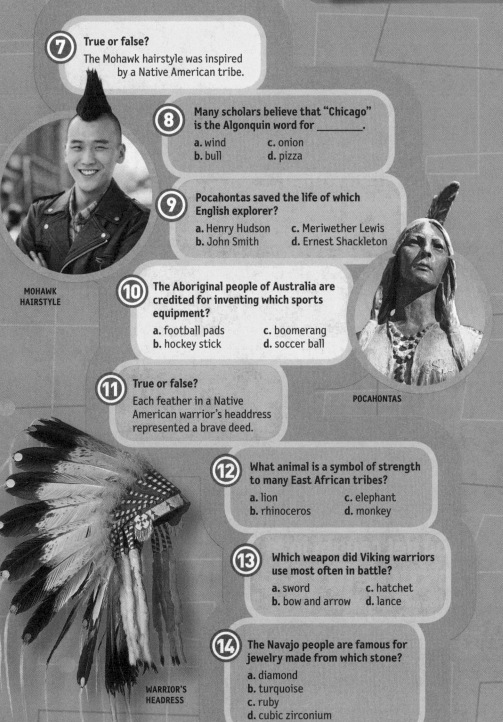

7 True or false?
The Mohawk hairstyle was inspired by a Native American tribe.

8 Many scholars believe that "Chicago" is the Algonquin word for _____.
a. wind   c. onion
b. bull   d. pizza

9 Pocahontas saved the life of which English explorer?
a. Henry Hudson   c. Meriwether Lewis
b. John Smith   d. Ernest Shackleton

10 The Aboriginal people of Australia are credited for inventing which sports equipment?
a. football pads   c. boomerang
b. hockey stick   d. soccer ball

11 True or false?
Each feather in a Native American warrior's headdress represented a brave deed.

12 What animal is a symbol of strength to many East African tribes?
a. lion   c. elephant
b. rhinoceros   d. monkey

13 Which weapon did Viking warriors use most often in battle?
a. sword   c. hatchet
b. bow and arrow   d. lance

14 The Navajo people are famous for jewelry made from which stone?
a. diamond
b. turquoise
c. ruby
d. cubic zirconium

MOHAWK HAIRSTYLE

POCAHONTAS

WARRIOR'S HEADRESS

145

CHECK YOUR ANSWERS ON PAGES 169–170.

SUMMER SURVIVAL KIT

1 If you've been stung by a jellyfish, which liquid should you wash the **infected** area with?

a. saltwater
b. chlorine
c. fresh water
d. chocolate milk

2 **True or false?**
Sparklers can reach temperatures hot enough to melt silver.

3 One symptom of Lyme disease—caused by tick bites—is a skin rash shaped like _____ .

a. a pyramid
b. a bullseye
c. a star
d. a happy face

4 Which clothing accessory is most likely to attract a **shark?**

a. a dark swimsuit
b. shiny jewelry
c. perfume
d. a giant shark costume

5 When tending a campfire, which of the following should you **never do?**

a. clear the area of any trash
b. use dead wood for the fire
c. leave the fire unattended
d. have water available

6 What should you do if you get caught in a **rip current?**

a. swim toward the shore
b. swim toward the sea
c. swim parallel to the shore
d. remain still

7 True or false?
A poison ivy rash is **contagious.**

8 What hours of the day are the sun's rays the **strongest?**

a. 6 p.m. to 12 a.m.   c. 2 p.m. to 6 p.m.
b. 10 a.m. to 2 p.m.   d. 7 p.m. to 12 a.m.

9 Which of the following foods is best to eat if you feel dehydrated?

a. ice cream   c. watermelon
b. pretzels   d. bread

10 Mosquitoes are most likely to breed in _____.

a. standing water   c. rotting fruit
b. trees   d. trash

11 What should you wear on your feet when riding a bike?

a. flip-flops   c. sneakers
b. cleats   d. sandals

12 Which food should you not keep outside for more than an hour on a scorching day?

a. bread   c. bananas
b. egg salad   d. a peanut-butter sandwich

A JELLYFISH OFF THE COAST OF MALAPASCUA, PHILIPPINES

13 Which of the following will not **protect** you from the sun's rays?

a. a long-sleeved shirt
b. swimming in the ocean
c. sunscreen
d. standing in the shade

CHECK YOUR ANSWERS ON PAGES 169–170.

TRUE or FALSE?
Going to Extremes

1 A LARGER VARIETY OF SPECIES OF WILDLIFE LIVE IN THE SAN DIEGO ZOO IN CALIFORNIA, U.S.A., THAN ANYWHERE ELSE ON EARTH.

2 DAREDEVIL FELIX BAUMGARTNER JUMPED FROM THE INTERNATIONAL SPACE STATION (ISS) TO ACHIEVE THE WORLD'S HIGHEST SKYDIVE.

3 ARICA IN CHILE RECEIVED NO RAINFALL FOR MORE THAN 14 YEARS.

4 THERE ARE MORE ACTIVE VOLCANOES IN THE UNITED STATES THAN IN ANY OTHER COUNTRY IN THE WORLD.

5 BUNGEE JUMPING WAS INSPIRED BY AN OLD HARVEST TRADITION IN THE SOUTH PACIFIC.

6 THE HABANERO IS THE WORLD'S HOTTEST PEPPER.

7 CHARLES LINDBERGH FLEW NONSTOP AROUND THE WORLD IN 1927.

8 THE RHINOCEROS BEETLE IS THE WORLD'S STRONGEST BEETLE.

9 THE NILE RIVER IS ALMOST TWICE THE LENGTH OF THE MISSISSIPPI RIVER.

10 IN 2011, 175 TORNADOES OCCURRED IN THE UNITED STATES OVER A 24-HOUR PERIOD.

11 THE LONGEST RUNNING RACE EVER RECORDED TOOK PLACE ACROSS AFRICA IN 1929.

12 A CAMEL CAN SURVIVE SEVERAL MONTHS WITHOUT FOOD.

13 IT TAKES THE INTERNATIONAL SPACE STATION 24 HOURS TO ORBIT EARTH.

14 COCKROACHES EXISTED DURING THE TIME OF DINOSAURS.

15 SOME SAND DUNES OF DASHT-ET LUT DESERT IN IRAN ARE TALLER THAN THE EIFFEL TOWER.

16 MICHIGAN STADIUM IN ANN ARBOR, MICHIGAN, U.S.A., IS SO LARGE THAT IT'S VISIBLE FROM SPACE.

17 BEFORE HALF-PIPES WERE INVENTED, SKATEBOARDERS PRACTICED RIDING IN EMPTY SWIMMING POOLS.

18 A VIOLENT STORM ON JUPITER HAS LASTED FOR AT LEAST THREE CENTURIES.

19 A PERSON IN ANCIENT MAYA WHO LOST IN A GAME OF RACQUETBALL WAS OFTEN SACRIFICED TO THE GODS.

20 THE LARGEST ICEBERG EVER RECORDED WAS AS BIG AS THE U.S. STATE OF TEXAS.

21 NORWEGIAN SCIENTIST THOR HEYERDAHL SAILED 4,300 MILES (6,920 KM) ACROSS THE PACIFIC ON A RAFT CALLED THE *KON-TIKI* FROM PERU TO POLYNESIA.

22 SOME TYPES OF SHARKS CAN LEAP UP TO 20 FEET (6 M) ABOVE THE OCEAN SURFACE.

23 ONLY THREE PEOPLE HAVE EVER BEEN TO THE DEEPEST POINT IN THE OCEAN.

24 IN 1989, PEOPLE IN RUSSIA SUCCEEDED IN DRILLING A HOLE TO THE CENTER OF EARTH.

25 THE SURFACE TEMPERATURES ON VENUS ARE HOT ENOUGH TO MELT LEAD.

26 SURFING WAS A SPORT RESERVED FOR ROYALTY IN ANCIENT HAWAII.

27 PEOPLE WHO HAVE CLIMBED THE "SEVEN SUMMITS" HAVE CLIMBED THE HIGHEST MOUNTAIN ON EACH CONTINENT.

28 MOTORCYCLE DAREDEVIL EVEL KNIEVEL IS BELIEVED TO HAVE BROKEN BONES IN HIS BODY MORE THAN 400 TIMES IN HIS LIFE.

29 THE BLUE WHALE CAN EAT ITS BODY WEIGHT IN FOOD IN A SINGLE DAY.

30 IN 1875, NAVAL OFFICER MATTHEW WEBB SMEARED PORPOISE OIL OVER HIS BODY SO THAT HE COULD SWIM AS QUICKLY AS POSSIBLE ACROSS THE ENGLISH CHANNEL.

CHECK YOUR ANSWERS ON PAGES 169–170.

AWESOME AUSTRALIA

2 Which city is the capital of Australia?
a. Canberra
b. Sydney
c. Melbourne
d. Perth

1 What mineral gives Ayers Rock, or Uluru, its **red** color?
a. zinc
b. iron
c. diamond
d. quartz

3 True or false? There are more sheep than people **living** in Australia.

4 **Vegemite**, a popular sandwich spread, is made from _____.
a. soybeans
b. brewer's yeast
c. chocolate
d. vanilla beans

5 Australia's national rugby team is named after which native animal?
a. echidna
b. platypus
c. wallaby
d. dingo

6 In Australia, "**outback**" refers to _____.
a. a restaurant
b. the desert
c. a backyard
d. the sky

7 What instrument has been used by the aboriginal people of Australia for at least **1,000** years?
a. piano
b. kazoo
c. accordion
d. didgerido

8 **True or false?**
Australia was colonized by **criminals** from England.

9 **Which plant is a koala's main source of food?**
a. bamboo
b. eucalyptus leaves
c. cactus spines
d. blackberries

10 What **currency** would you use to pay for something in Australia?
a. Australian dollar
b. yen
c. pound
d. Monopoly money

11 The **roof** design of the Sydney Opera House was inspired by _____.
a. an orange peel
b. a seashell
c. an Egyptian pyramid
d. Sonic the Hedgehog

12 "Sunnies" is Aussie slang for _____.
a. clouds
b. baseball
c. sunglasses
d. sisters

13 What is "footy"?
a. a person who loves food
b. a type of football
c. a measuring stick
d. a hot dog

14 What is a common **burger** topping in Australia?
a. beets
b. carrots
c. celery
d. broccoli

AYERS ROCK/ULURU

ODD SPORTS

ZIP-LINING

1 Which of the following sports is an Olympic event?

a. water-skiing   c. ziplining
b. race walking   d. ballroom dancing

2 True or false?
A sumo wrestler automatically wins if he stomps his feet louder than his opponent.

3 In the French martial art *canne de combat*, opponents battle one another using _____.

a. lightsabers   c. cans
b. pillows   d. walking sticks

4 During a swimming obstacle-course event in the 1900 Olympics, swimmers had to do all of the following except _____.

a. swim a 100-yard (91.4-m) race   c. crawl over a boat
b. climb a pole   d. jump a hurdle

5 Before a horse competes in a dressage event, its mane and tail are usually _____.

a. braided   c. teased
b. cut off   d. curled

6 In curling, a "burned stone" is the name for a stone that has _____.

a. been set on fire
b. broken
c. been touched by a teammate
d. flown into the crowd

CURLING

7 Each year, teams from all over the world gather to play which fictional sport involving broomsticks?

a. the Hunger Games **c.** podracing
b. Quidditch **d.** airball

8 Which animals once competed in an Olympic long-jump event?

a. cats **c.** horses
b. kangaroos **d.** dolphins

9 "Lady Shatterly," "Admiral Attackbar," and "Mad Mel Arena" are nicknames of athletes who compete in _____ .

a. roller derby **c.** water polo
b. figure skating **d.** race-car driving

10 True or false?
Painting was once an Olympic sport.

11 What sport, which usually involves more than one person, became a solo event in the 1984 Olympic Games?

a. ice dancing
b. synchronized swimming
c. wrestling
d. soccer

ARTIST'S PALETTE

12 What sport, which usually involves only one person, became a pairs event in the 2000 Olympic Games?

a. diving **c.** speed skating
b. trampoline **d.** weight lifting

13 What gym-class exercise was an Olympic sport in 1896?

a. sit-ups **c.** rope climbing
b. push-ups **d.** jump rope

TRAMPOLINING

CHECK YOUR ANSWERS ON PAGES 169–170.

MAP MANIA!

ON SAFARI

ARCTIC OCEAN

NORTH AMERICA

PACIFIC OCEAN

ATLANTIC OCEAN

E

A

F

SOUTH AMERICA

When most people hear the word "safari," they think of Africa. That's because Africa has many countries where you can go to see animals in the wild. But other places have safaris, too. Answer these questions. Then match each safari to its location on the map.

1 INDIA

Head to Periyar National Park for a glimpse of wild Asian elephants. On a hot day, you'll find these animals cooling off by the water and fanning themselves with their _____.

a. feet   **c.** ears
b. trunks   **d.** tails

2 BRAZIL

The Pantanal—a large wetland in Brazil—is home to many jaguars. The spots on jaguars are called rosettes because _____.

a. they smell like roses
b. they are shaped like roses
c. they are rose colored
d. roses are the jaguar's favorite flower

3 GALÁPAGOS ISLANDS

Blue-footed boobies can be found on the Galápagos Islands. When European colonists saw how clumsy this bird is on land, they named it after the Spanish word for_____.

a. fool   **c.** dancer
b. balance   **d.** quiet

154

World of ADVENTURE

4. SWITZERLAND

In the Swiss National Park, you can see many animals, including the Alpine ibex, which is a type of _____.

a. bison
b. goat
c. rabbit
d. cow

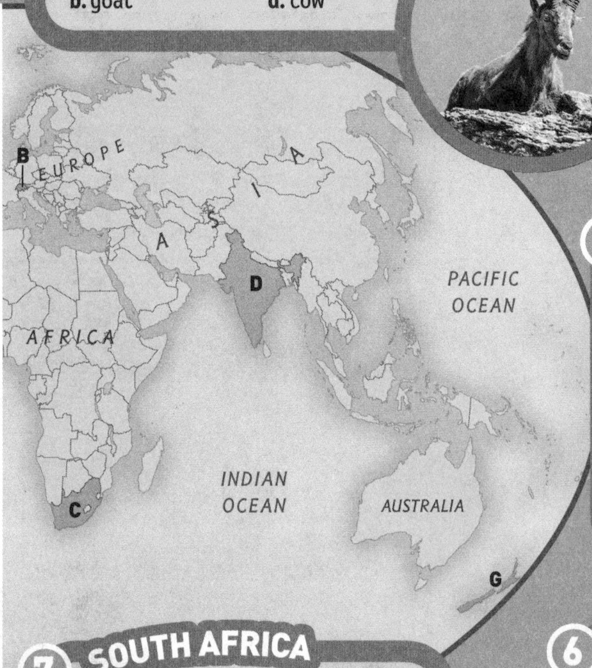

5. CANADA

Travel to Bay du Nord Wilderness Reserve in Newfoundland, Canada, to see the woodland caribou. The caribou travel together in groups called _____.

a. schools
b. flocks
c. gaggles
d. herds

Map labels: B EUROPE, A ASIA, D, AFRICA, C, INDIAN OCEAN, AUSTRALIA, PACIFIC OCEAN, G

7. SOUTH AFRICA

The Jukani Wildlife Sanctuary is home to many animals—including the African lion. Male lions have bushy manes for all of the following reasons except _____.

a. to attract mates
b. to protect their necks
c. to intimidate other males
d. that they're too lazy to cut it

6. NEW ZEALAND

The Willowbank Wildlife Reserve in New Zealand boasts plenty of wildlife. This includes the kiwi—a small bird that is unable to fly and is related to the _____.

a. ostrich
b. parrot
c. hummingbird
d. eagle

8–14

MATCH EACH HIGHLIGHTED AREA ON THE MAP WITH THE PLACES MENTIONED IN THE QUESTIONS ABOVE.

CHECK YOUR ANSWERS ON PAGES 169–170.

GAME SHOW

ULTIMATE ADVENTURE CHALLENGE

1 What object from nature was the inspiration for the Native American dreamcatcher?

a. caterpillar cocoon
b. bird's nest
c. spiderweb
d. tortoise shell

2 TRUE OR FALSE?

The name of the winter sport "skeleton" is inspired by the bone-chilling track on which athletes ride their sleds.

3 TRUE OR FALSE?

The tallest drop-tower ride—Zumanjaro: Drop of Doom—is taller than the Statue of Liberty.

4 What name is an Aboriginal word for boomerang?

a. Dan
b. Francesca
c. Christopher
d. Kylie

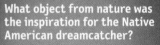

5 If you are at the beach, do not go into the water if you see a _____ nearby.

a. green flag
b. blue flag
c. white flag
d. red flag

6 In December 2013, England's Prince Harry battled gusty winds and freezing temperatures during a trek to which destination?

a. Miami, Florida, U.S.A.
b. South Pole, Antarctica
c. London, England
d. Reykjavik, Iceland

7 Each year, almost one million people travel to the Andes Mountains in Peru to see which cultural site?

a. Iguazu Falls   c. Machu Picchu
b. Chichen Itza   d. Dinosaur Museum

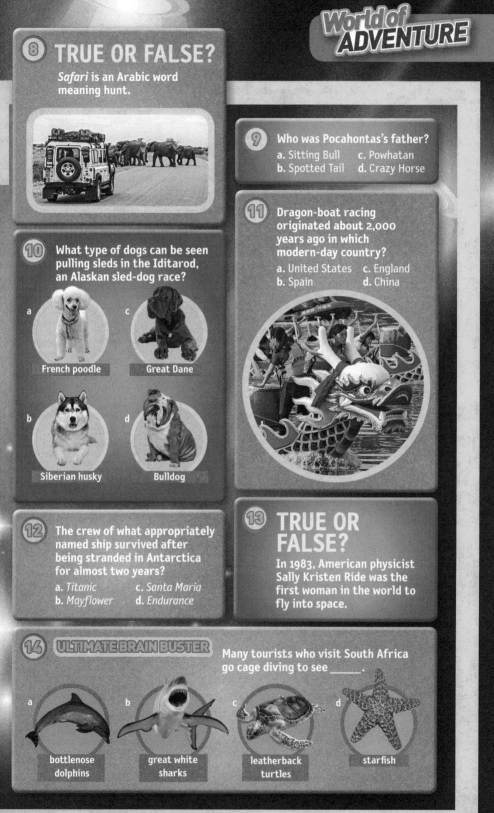

8 TRUE OR FALSE?

Safari is an Arabic word meaning hunt.

9 Who was Pocahontas's father?

a. Sitting Bull c. Powhatan
b. Spotted Tail d. Crazy Horse

10 What type of dogs can be seen pulling sleds in the Iditarod, an Alaskan sled-dog race?

a
French poodle

c
Great Dane

b
Siberian husky

d
Bulldog

11 Dragon-boat racing originated about 2,000 years ago in which modern-day country?

a. United States c. England
b. Spain d. China

12 The crew of what appropriately named ship survived after being stranded in Antarctica for almost two years?

a. *Titanic* c. *Santa Maria*
b. *Mayflower* d. *Endurance*

13 TRUE OR FALSE?

In 1983, American physicist Sally Kristen Ride was the first woman in the world to fly into space.

14 ULTIMATE BRAIN BUSTER

Many tourists who visit South Africa go cage diving to see _____.

a
bottlenose dolphins

b
great white sharks

c
leatherback turtles

d
starfish

CHECK YOUR ANSWERS ON PAGES 169–170.

ANSWERS

Wild WORLD

On the Farm, pages 10–11

1. **True.** Chickens can fly, but most can fly only short distances.
2. b   3. d   4. b   5. c   6. a
7. a   8. c   9. c   10. d
11. **True.** The feathers are used to make pillows, mattresses, and down coverings.
12. a

Call of the Wild, pages 12–13

1. d
2. **True.** Cheetahs chirp and purr but can't roar.
3. d   4. c   5. a   6. c   7. c
8. **True.** Fireflies flash in patterns to communicate with one another.
9. a   10. b
11. **False.** Scientists know a lot about dolphin communication, but the meaning of most dolphin chirps and squeaks are still a mystery.
12. b   13. a   14. d
15. **False.** Birds repeat the same calls and songs again and again.

What a Hoot! pages 14–15

1. d   2. b   3. a
4. **False.** Some owls, including the snowy owl, also hunt during the day.
5. c   6. b   7. c
8. **True.** Owls can't move their eyes, but they can twist their heads 270 degrees.
9. d   10. a   11. a   12. b
13. b   14. b
15. **False.** Baby owls are called owlets.

Time for a Change, pages 16–17

1. c   2. a
3. **True.** A grown-up flounder lies flat against the seafloor with both eyes on its upper surface for vision. As the fish grows, an eye moves from its underside to topside.
4. b   5. b   6. d   7. b   8. c
9. **False.** Dogs' fur actually helps them keep cool in the summer and helps prevent bug bites and sunburn.
10. a   11. d

12. **True.** Penguins aren't waterproof while molting, so they can't swim to catch fish to eat.
13. a   14. c   15. c

Purrfect Cats, pages 18–19

1. d   2. a   3. a   4. c   5. b
6. b
7. **True.** Cats can't digest plants.
8. a   9. d   10. a   11. c
12. **False.** The endangered Asian lion lives in the Gir Forest in India.
13. d

Map Mania! Animal Invaders, pages 20–21

1. c   2. b   3. d
4. **True.** This didn't work because the rats come out at night, and mongooses hunt during the day!
5. c
6. **b.** Washing mussels off boats before the boats are taken to other lakes will also help.
7. **1, B** Australia
8. **2, D** Florida, U.S.A./Puerto Rico
9. **3, E** Hong Kong, Papua, Mauritius, Palau
10. **4, C** Hawaii, U.S.A.
11. **5, A** South Africa
12. **6, F** Great Lakes region, U.S.A.–Canada

The Ice Age, pages 22–23

1. d
2. **False.** Mammoths were larger than mastodons and had different teeth.
3. c   4. b   5. c
6. **False.** Ice covered a larger portion of planet Earth, but there were still plenty of forests, oceans, lakes, and rivers.
7. c   8. a   9. b   10. a
11. **True.** Camelops, a camel relative, lived in western North America during the Ice Age.
12. b   13. b   14. c
15. **True.** Humans may have used dogs to help bring down the giant, elephant-like creatures.

Hip Hopper, pages 24–25

1. **False.** Kangaroos hop everywhere! They can't run.
2. b   3. c
4. **False.** A kangaroo's maximum speed is 35 miles an hour (56 km/h)—which is still very fast.
5. c   6. b   7. b
8. **False.** A kangaroo uses its tail for balance.
9. d
10. **True.** The newborn grows its powerful hind legs while in the mother's pouch.
11. b   12. d   13. a   14. a   15. c

Animal Architects, pages 26–27

1. a   2. c   3. b   4. c   5. b
6. a
7. **True.** Cathedral termite mounds may be 15 feet (4.6 m) tall!
8. **True.** During strong winds, one or two strands may break, but the web usually survives.
9. d
10. d   11. a
12. **True.** Chimpanzees weave together living branches to make their nests, spending 10 minutes building a new nest every night.

True or False? It's a Jungle, pages 28–29

1. **False.** The Barbary macaque has almost no tail. It is also the only species of monkey that lives in the wild in Europe.
2. **False.** Tigers live in jungles, forests, grasslands, and swamps across parts of Asia.
3. **True.** There are more ants in the rain forest than any other creature.
4. **True.** Illegal hunting and the destruction of rain forest habitat has endangered most species of lemurs.
5. **True.** The okapi lives in the rain forest in the Democratic Republic of the Congo in Africa.
6. **False.** The Amazon in South America is the world's largest rain forest.
7. **True.** The fungus has killed frogs in the rain forests of Australia, Panama, and other countries.
8. **True.** Many rain forest plant and insect species have not yet been discovered!
9. **False.** An orchid is a type of flower that grows in the rain forest.
10. **True.** Since 1979, the dry season in the Amazon has gotten several weeks longer.
11. **True.** Your house cat may hate water, but jaguars often swim while hunting.
12. **True.** The area of a rain forest formed by the treetops is called the canopy. Many animals live there.
13. **False.** There is a large rain forest in Central Africa.
14. **False.** The quetzal is a colorful bird that lives in the rain forests of Central America.
15. **False.** Skunks live in Canada, the United States, and northern Mexico.
16. **True.** The baby snakes turn green 6 to 12 months later.
17. **True.** The civet, a small rain forest mammal, eats coffee berries, and the beans come out in its poopages. People pay a lot of money for "civet coffee"!
18. **False.** Sloths are actually related to armadillos and anteaters.
19. **True.** The process of cutting down rain forests is called deforestation. This causes animals to lose their sources of food and shelter.
20. **False.** Pineapples grow on the ground from a stalk in dry, tropical areas.
21. **True.** Asian elephants live in the jungles of India, Thailand, Nepal, Vietnam, and other countries.
22. **True.** If you get a parrot as a pet, be prepared to keep it for a long time!
23. **True.** Spider monkeys also eat fruit, nuts, leaves, and bird eggs.

24. **True.** Nectar bats feed at night, just like other bats do.
25. **False.** Many non-poisonous frogs look as bright and colorful as their toxic relatives! This helps trick predators!
26. **True.** Some Australian plants are related to species that lived more than 100 million years ago.
27. **False.** Toucans do have huge beaks, but they are only about a third of the length of the bird's body.
28. **False.** Though smaller than their African cousins, Borneo's pygmy elephants are still big: about 8 feet (2.4 m) tall.
29. **True.** An endangered crab lives in tree holes in the rain forest of West Africa.
30. **False.** The boa can be 13 feet (4 m) long, but the anaconda is even bigger—it grows up to 30 feet (9 m).

Game Show: Ultimate Animal Challenge, pages 30–31

1. c
2. **True.** The squid turns red to attract females and white to tell other males to go away.
3. a 4. c 5. a 6. d
7. b 8. b 9. d 10. a
11. **False.** *Tyrannosaurus rex* went extinct millions of years before the Ice Age.
12. c 13. b
14. **True.** Hairs on the spider's body trap air so it can breathe underwater for a short time.
15. c

SCORING

0–56
HORSING AROUND
The wild world is full of surprises. You may not be an animal expert, but you're not afraid of guessing and taking risks. You might become a cowgirl or cowboy someday!

57–112
TALKING TURKEY
You're totally serious about animals and would go out of your way to rescue a lost cat or dog or to help a turtle cross the road. Keep it up and you'll have a house full of pets when you grow up!

113–169
COWABUNGA!
What an animal brainiac! You know a wallaroo from a wallaby, an alligator from a crocodile from a caiman, and an aardvark from an anteater from an armadillo. You'll likely have a new species named after you someday.

Around the GLOBE

Exploring Niagara Falls, pages 34–35
1. d
2. **True.** It was founded in 1885.
3. b 4. d 5. a 6. c
7. b 8. c 9. b
10. **False.** There are about 500 waterfalls that are "taller" than Niagara. At its highest point, Horseshoe Falls is about 180 feet (55 m) high.
11. a 12. d 13. c
14. **True.** For a very brief time in late March 1848, strong westerly winds and an ice jam near Buffalo prevented water from reaching Niagara Falls.

Nation Nicknames, pages 36–37
1. c 2. b 3. b
4. **True.** Mongolia is also known as the Land of the Blue Sky.

5. c 6. d 7. a
8. **False.** Japan is known as the Land of the Rising Sun.
9. c 10. a 11. d 12. b
13. **True.** Canada is also known as the Great White North.

On the Move, pages 38–39
1. a 2. d 3. c 4. b 5. b
6. b 7. a 8. d
9. **False.** Matatus are decorated minibuses used in Kenya.
10. **True.** Seaplanes often get people from the international airport in Male to other islands in the Maldives.
11. **False.** Feluccas are traditional boats sailed on the Nile.

True or False? Pack Your Bags! pages 40–41
1. **True.** It's also true that here shaking one's head means "yes."
2. **False.** That honor goes to Hong Kong.
3. **False.** At over 14,000 feet (4,267 m) above sea level, it is in Tibet.
4. **False.** At 125,566 miles (202,080 km), Canada has the world's longest coastline.
5. **True.** The Iolani Palace was home to several members of Hawaii's monarchy.
6. **False.** Vatican City's coins can be used in Italy and the European Union.

7. **True.** Mexico City was built on an unstable lake bed.

8. **False.** The T Express at Everland in South Korea wins this contest.

9. **True.** It also has lots of orchids and a 16-foot (4.9-m) "Green Wall."

10. **True.** They are located outside of Paris, in Hong Kong, and outside Tokyo.

11. **False.** Europe's most visited zoo is Berlin's, hosting more than 3 million tourists each year.

12. **False.** London had the world's first subway, opening in 1863. Budapest, Hungary was second and Paris third.

13. **True.** Dole Plantation has this maze, made up of over 14,000 Hawaiian plants.

14. **False.** This national park has more than a million flamingo residents.

15. **True.** The airport is about 300 square miles (777 sq. km), while Bahrain's area is 293 square miles (759 sq km).

16. **True.** Ski Dubai offers all these attractions, even if it's 100°F (37.8°C) outside.

17. **False.** The British Museum's collection has 8 million objects, so it would take more than 30 years.

18. **True.** The concrete Big Banana near Coffs Harbor is 36 feet (11 m) long and 16.4 feet (5 m) high.

19. **True.** Glamping is a term made by combining the words "glamorous" and "camping."

20. **False.** The three airstrips serving McMurdo Station are made of snow or ice.

21. **True.** This eco-lodge is largely made of wood and straw.

22. **False.** Namibia's canyon is the second largest in the world, after the Grand Canyon.

23. **True.** This rule even applies to French fries.

24. **False.** The ride is located at WhiteWater World in Australia. (Wedgie riders go from 0 to 28 miles an hour (45 km/h) in two seconds.)

25. **True.** 16.8 million visitors came to London in 201

26. **False.** Yellowstone National Park, U.S.A., established in 1872, is the oldest.

27. **True.** This airport also has a 3-D cinema for entertainment.

28. **False.** Both sun bears and orangutans are native to Southeast Asia, not Central America.

29. **True.** The museum also has collections of washing machines and brooms.

30. **True.** This is enough rooms to house every person who lives in Atlanta, Denver, Miami, San Francisco, and Washington, D.C., combined.

Sweet Treats, pages 42–43

1. **b**
2. **True.** Ice Cream City in Tokyo offers more than 300 different flavors.
3. **d**   4. **c**   5. **a**
6. **True.** There are also cantaloupe and tomato flavors for fruit-loving caramel eaters.
7. **c**   8. **a**   9. **d**   10. **c**
11. **False.** People in Finland eat this soup. It is made from a relative of the blueberry called a bilberry.

It's the Law! pages 44–45

1. **b**   2. **c**
3. **True.** Even taking a sip of water is against the law—and rule breakers are fined 85 euros (about $110).
4. **b**   5. **d**   6. **b**
7. **True.** Wrestling with bears is also illegal in this state.
8. **d**   9. **c**   10. **b**   11. **d**
12. **True.** It's also against the law to hold hands or swear in public here.
13. **c**

On Your Marks, pages 46–47

1. **b**   2. **a**
3. **True.** This 1,107-yard (1,012-m) race takes place in England. (It began about 50 years ago.)
4. **a**   5. **a**   6. **d**   7. **d**
8. **c**   9. **c**   10. **b**
11. **True.** This competition takes place in Sonkajärvi, Finland.

Map Mania! Flags of the World, pages 48–49

1. Barbados	13. **A**, Zambia
2. Canada	14. **B**, Seychelles
3. Guyana	15. **C**, Latvia
4. Andorra	16. **D**, Mongolia
5. Latvia	17. **E**, Australia
6. Bahrain	18. **F**, Bahrain
7. Cameroon	19. **G**, Canada
8. North Korea	20. **H**, Guyana
9. Seychelles	21. **I**, Barbados
10. Mongolia	22. **J**, Andorra
11. Australia	23. **K**, North Korea
12. Zambia	24. **L**, Cameroon

Game Show: Ultimate Geography Challenge, pages 50–51

1. **a**
2. **True.** Railroad-style crossing gates hold cars back whenever a plane lands or departs.
3. **a**   4. **c**   5. **d**   6. **d**
7. **b**   8. **d**   9. **a**
10. **False.** This is the description of Bhutan's flag. China's flag is red with five gold stars.
11. **c**   12. **b**   13. **c**
14. **True.** These yellow taxis are open-air and seat two people.
15. **a**

160

SCORING

0–44
WHERE IN THE WORLD
You're still learning to find your way around the globe, but you'll get there in the end. Try watching travel documentaries and reading guidebooks and atlases to learn about countries of the world.

45–90
COUNTRY WISEGUY
You love traveling and going on adventures in foreign lands: *Around the World in 80 Days* is your movie of choice! Keep a record of your journeys and take videos of new places you visit, and one day you'll become the go-to travel agent.

91–142
TERRIFIC TRAILBLAZER
You're always the first to arrive! You're an expert at deciphering travel timetables, reading maps, and orienteering. You'll likely be an explorer one day. Your friends and family can certainly learn a lot from you—at least about quizzes.

Pop CULTURE

On the Job, pages 54–55
1. c   2. d   3. b   4. a   5. a
6. a   7. c   8. c   9. a   10. b
11. c   12. b   13. c   14. a

Page-Turners, pages 56–57
1. b   2. d   3. a   4. a
5. c   6. d   7. c
8. **False.** The Tucks remain young by drinking water from a special spring.
9. a   10. d   11. c
12. **True.** Count Olaf poses as a distant relative so that he can steal the children's fortune.
13. c   14. d

True or False? Heroes and Villains, pages 58–59
1. **False.** Luke's father, Anakin Skywalker, became Darth Vader.
2. **False.** Snow White falls into a deep sleep by eating a poisonous apple. Sleeping Beauty pricks her finger on a spinning wheel.
3. **True.** Bambi and other deer are threatened by "man" throughout the story, and his mother is killed by a human hunter.
4. **True.** King Pig is often the last pig standing in the game.
5. **False.** Count Dracula lives in a castle in Transylvania, a region in Romania.
6. **True.** Fawful, a character from the Beanbean Kingdom, appears as a villain in most games from the Mario and Luigi series.
7. **False.** Miss Hannigan treats Annie poorly.
8. **True.** Although the Grinch succeeds in stealing the gifts and decorations, the Whos of Whoville remain cheerful.
9. **True.** Anyone who looked at Medusa and her hair of snakes would be turned into stone.
10. **False.** Bilbo Baggins must reclaim the kingdom from a dragon named Smaug.
11. **True.** Captain Jack Sparrow is forced onto Blackbeard's ship while the legendary pirate searches for the Fountain of Youth.
12. **True.** In most Legend of Zelda games, Link must save Princess Zelda from Ganondorf.
13. **False.** The vengeful pirate is named Captain Hook.
14. **False.** Death Eaters are followers of Voldemort. Voldemort is sometimes referred to as He Who Must Not Be Named.
15. **True.** In both tales, the wolf tries to eat the main characters.
16. **False.** Oz is terrorized by the Wicked Witch of the West. The White Witch wreaks havoc on the land of Narnia.
17. **True.** Conflicting beliefs about mutants and humans eventually made them enemies.
18. **False.** Dr. Jekyll transforms into the evil Mr. Hyde after taking a potion.
19. **False.** Lex Luthor tries to destroy Superman with Kryptonite.
20. **False.** Cruella de Vil kidnaps the puppies because she hopes to use them for their fur.

21. **False.** The "Z" in Professor Z stands for Zündapp, which is also the car model of the character.
22. **True.** Percy must find the Golden Fleece to restore a magical tree back to health.
23. **True.** In the previous movie, Blu hooks a fire extinguisher to Nigel's leg and sets it off, causing Nigel to fly out of the plane and into the propeller.
24. **True.** Doctor Eggman, the main villain in the series, wants to conquer the world to build the Eggman Empire.
25. **True.** Fortunately, Mowgli is saved by other animals in the jungle.
26. **False.** Gru is recruited to find a stolen secret laboratory containing a powerful mutagen PX-41.
27. **True.** The torn dress is later transformed into a beautiful ball gown by Cinderella's Fairy Godmother.
28. **False.** Stuart, who is a mouse, must watch out for the family cat, Snowbell. The two eventually become friends.

29. **False.** Matilda admires Miss Honey but dislikes Miss Trunchbull, whom she often plays tricks on.
30. **True.** The eels, whose electricity has been artificially charged, attack Max Dillon and turn him into a living electric generator called Electro.

You Can Dance! pages 60–61

1. c
2. **False.** Though some people believe that the name of the dance was inspired by Charles Lindbergh, the dance itself was created by George "Shorty" Snowden, a U.S. dancer of the 1920s and 1930s.
3. c   4. a   5. a   6. c   7. d

8. **True.** The dance involved forming fists with your hands and then moving them in a circular manner.
9. c   10. b   11. d   12. a
13. c   14. a

Mad for the Movies, pages 62–63

1. b   2. a
3. **False.** E.T. uses a game called *Speak & Spell* to phone home.
4. c   5. a   6. d   7. b
8. **False.** Aladdin is the name of the character who unleashes the genie from a lamp.
9. c   10. d   11. b   12. d
13. a   14. b

Game Show: Ultimate Pop Culture Challenge, pages 64–65

1. b   2. c
3. **b.** Dr. Who is a Time Lord: Chronometers are precision timekeepers, such as a pilot's wristwatch.
4. a   5. d
6. **False.** The dance originated in Cuba in the 1930s and it has never been banned.
7. c   8. c   9. b   10. a
11. b   12. d   13. d   14. b

SCORING

0–32
GET THE VIBES
You may not have your finger permanently on the pulse or be a trendsetter or fashionista, but you're up to date with the latest movies, videos, and games.

33–65
REALLY COOL
Popular culture is your thing, but you are not stuck in front of the computer or TV or constantly playing with your smartphone. You're often out and about enjoying the rich tapestry of life.

66–100
STAR QUALITIES
If there was a competition about celebrity gossip, you would be the winner. And people come to you to know all about the latest electronic gadgets and upcoming movies. You are a glittering success.

Back to NATURE

What a Gem, pages 68–69

1. a   2. b   3. b   4. d
5. b   6. c
7. **False.** Some sapphires are orange, yellow, or even pink!
8. c
9. **b.** In fact, The gem "garnet" got its name from the Latin word for "pomegranate."
10. **True.** On the scale of mineral hardness, diamond is at the top!
11. a   12. c   13. d
14. **True.** Chinese kings were often buried with jade ornaments.
15. d

Nature's Greatest Hits, pages 70–71

1. a
2. **True.** Gases full of sulfur coming from the volcano burst into blue flames when they meet the air.
3. c   4. c   5. d   6. b
7. **a.** The Colorado River carved through the rock over millions of years.
8. **False.** When the moon is full, you may be able to see a faint lunar rainbow, or "moonbow."
9. b   10. b   11. a   12. d   13. a

In Bloom, pages 72–73

1. d   2. a
3. **False.** Some species of bamboo produce flowers every year, while others flower just once every 100 years!
4. c   5. d   6. b
7. **True.** Sunflowers can grow up to 12 feet (3.6 m) tall.
8. b   9. d   10. a
11. c   12. c   13. c
14. **True.** Several different flower varieties smell like chocolate, including chocolate chip bugleweed and frosted chocolate viola.

Map Mania! Fantastic Forests pages 74–75

1. c   2. d   3. b   4. a
5. d   Most agree that people forced the trees to grow like that, perhaps for use in furniture- or boat-making.
6. c   7. 1B   8. 2F   9. 3D
10. 4C   11. 5A   12. 6E

Life's a Beach, pages 76–77

1. d
2. **False.** Although sand does contain bits of seashells, most sand grains are tiny pieces of rock.
3. b   4. b   5. a   6. c
7. **True.** Some beaches have just one high tide each day while others have two.
8. b   9. c   10. d   11. b   12. d

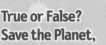

True or False? Save the Planet, pages 78–79

1. **False.** It depends how long you stay in the shower! A ten-minute shower uses about the same amount of water as a bath.
2. **True.** Some species are naturally rare, but many are rare due to human activities.
3. **False.** Global warming has caused average ocean temperatures to increase.
4. **True.** In the 1960s, fewer than 100 one-horned rhinos remained. Now, they number more than 500.
5. **False.** In 2000, about 6 billion people lived on Earth.
6. **False.** Some elephants are born without tusks, and an elephant can survive if its tusks are removed. Still, most poachers kill an elephant to take its tusks.
7. **True.** The first Earth Day was celebrated in 1970.
8. **False.** This is a made-up word. The correct term is environmentalist!
9. **True.** About 30 percent of that garbage gets recycled or composted.
10. **False.** Siberian tigers live in Eastern Russia through parts of China and North Korea.
11. **False.** New Delhi in India is the world's most polluted city.
12. **False.** A refrigerator uses about five times as much power as a TV.
13. **True.** Habitat destruction is the number one reason that so many animals are endangered.
14. **False.** A poacher is a person who hunts and kills animals that are protected by laws.
15. **True.** If you don't rinse the dishes beforehand, then the dishwasher uses about 35 percent less water.

16. **True.** We are losing animal and plant species much faster than normal.
17. **True.** Fish accidentally eat tiny fragments of plastic that float around in the ocean.
18. **True.** DiCaprio also drives an electric car.
19. **True.** The law helps to protect the environment.
20. **False.** Global warming has caused the deaths of many corals.
21. **True.** A plastic cup takes about 450 years to break down.
22. **False.** The United States uses up more water per person than any other country.
23. **True.** Recycling rates have been rising ever since!
24. **True.** The only way to keep a TV from leaking extra energy is to unplug it.
25. **False.** Many fish species are endangered, including the bluefin tuna.
26. **False.** Some parrots are still caught in the wild, often illegally. Others are bred in captivity.
27. **True.** It takes 101 ounces (3 L) of water to manufacture a 34-ounce (1-L) water bottle.
28. **True.** Nearly 35 percent of amphibian species are endangered.
29. **False.** In 2012, about 27 percent of all waste was paper or cardboard, and just 13 percent was plastic.
30. **False.** Whalers used to hunt humpbacks, but the species has been protected and growing since the 1960s.

The Spa Treatment, pages 80–81

1. b   2. d
3. **False.** Minerals in the water turn it a milky blue color.
4. **False.** The temperature is about 106°F (41°C).
5. a   6. c   7. d   8. d
9. c   10. a   11. b   12. a
13. **True.** "Blood pond" is one of many different pools at Beppu Hot Spring in Japan.
14. d

Game Show: Ultimate Nature Challenge, pages 82–83

1. c   2. a
3. **True.** If snakes got loose in Hawaii, they could kill native wildlife.
4. **b.** The top of Mount Everest used to be at the bottom of a prehistoric ocean!
5. d
6. **True.** A rainbow has millions of distinct colors—and many are outside of the range of human vision.
7. d   8. c   9. c
10. **False.** Most lightning bolts flash from cloud to cloud and never hit the ground.
11. a   12. c   13. a
14. **True.** Scientists can only estimate the numbers of sand grains and stars, but the universe is so gigantic that stars win easily.
15. **a.** The egg case belongs to a skate, a type of fish that looks like a stingray.

SCORING

0–40

Buried in the Sand

All of nature is out there, waiting for you to discover it. Get your toes muddy, your hands dirty, and your hair full of spiderwebs, and you'll be on your way to a career as a park ranger.

41–80

Rock Solid

You've got a knack for understanding the world around you. You pay attention and notice everything from the petals on a daisy to the variety of gemstones. You'll make a great teacher or researcher.

81–125

Diamond in the Rough

Shine on! You aced this quiz, and you'll continue to succeed at whatever you set your mind to. The world needs more geologists, biologists, zoologists, ornithologists, and environmentalists.

The Rest Is HISTORY

Follow the Leader, pages 86–87

1. c
2. **True.** Called a semipresidential government, countries such as France, Finland, and Mongolia have both a president and a prime minister.
3. c   4. b   5. d   6. b   7. d
8. **False.** Ping is not a Chinese dynasty.
9. c   10. d   11. b   12. c   13. b
14. **True.** In 2009, Greenlanders voted for home rule and became a country within the kingdom of Denmark.

Secrets of the Sphinx, pages 88–89

1. a
2. **True.** Its head is about 70 feet (21.3 m) high.
3. b
4. **True.** It measures 240 feet (73.2 m) long and 66 feet (20 m) high.
5. c   6. d   7. a   8. b   9. b
10. **False.** Other sphinxes have the head of a ram instead of a man.
11. a   12. c
13. **True.** The workers' diet showed they weren't slaves. Regular people may have taken turns working out of duty to their leader.

Cool Critters, pages 90–91

1. c   2. b   3. c   4. a
5. c   6. a   7. b   8. c
9. **True.** He saw that finches adapted differently to the different environments in which they lived.
10. b
11. **True.** The legend is that if the ravens leave, it will be the end of the British Empire.

Ahoy, Matey, pages 92–93

1. b
2. **False.** "Ahoy, Matey" means "Hello, friend."
3. c   4. b   5. d
6. **True.** Francis Drake worked as a privateer for the queen, instructed to explore and secure lands in North America, mostly from Spanish colonists, and to raid Spanish ships.
7. **False.** A spanker is the biggest sail at the stern of a ship.
8. **d.** It is now often used to mean "prepare for a fight."
9. a   10. c   11. d
12. **False.** Anne Bonny and Mary Read were two female pirates who operated at the same time as Blackbeard. There have been other female pirates throughout history.
13. c

Game Night, pages 94–95

1. **True.** Senet has been around for thousands of years.
2. b   3. b   4. d   5. a
6. d   7. b   8. c   9. d
10. a   11. c   12. a
13. **True.** Also known as knucklebones, jacks was probably first played in Ancient Greece 2,000 years ago.

True or False? They Did *What?* pages 96–97

1. **False.** Columbus, and most people of his time, knew the world was round; however, he believed it was smaller than it really was.
2. **False.** Seward's bad investment was the purchase of Alaska. Despite the bargain price of $2 per acre, most of Congress and members of the press thought of Alaska as a huge frozen wasteland. Alaska is one-fifth the size of the rest of the United States and rich in natural resources. Its purchase has proved to be a wise one.
3. **True.** Ads were created for the foot powder during the campaign. One message was *"Vote for any candidate, but if you want well-being and hygiene, vote for Pulvapies."* There were enough write-in votes to elect the foot powder!
4. **False.** The Native Americans accepted objects to the value of $24 from Dutch governor Peter Minuit as gifts. But when the land was demanded, fighting broke out between the Native Americans and settlers, causing the deaths of more than 1,000 people (settlers and Native Americans). The fighting shows that the Native Americans did not knowingly enter into any contractual agreement with the Dutch.
5. **True.** In about 1870, Joseph Lister was the first doctor to sterilize his equipment and prove to other doctors that they could save lives with sterile conditions in operating rooms.
6. **True.** The use of metric instead of imperial measurement systems made it impossible to transfer information from a spacecraft team in Denver, Colorado, U.S.A., to a lab in California, U.S.A.
7. **True.** On its way from England to the United States, the ship hit an iceberg and sank. More than 1,500 people perished at sea.
8. **False.** Most of Napoleon's army died due to freezing temperatures and food shortages.

9. **False.** Much to its regret, Decca did turn down the Beatles; instead, they signed another music group called Brian Poole and the Tremeloes. One Direction signed with Syco Records.

10. **True.** The Bloomsbury chairman's eight-year-old daughter persuaded the publisher to accept it. Good thing he listened to her!

11. **False.** Troy was at war with Greece not Egypt. The Trojan Horse was filled with Greek soldiers.

12. **False.** The Hindenburg was filled with hydrogen, a flammable gas, which led to its eventual destruction in 1937.

13. **True.** Alexander's generals carved up his empire among themselves.

14. **True.** When Fleming returned to his lab, he saw that a blue mold had killed all the bacteria it had come into contact with. Penicillin is an unexpected by-product of the mold.

15. **True.** Wright tried to make an artificial rubber. It was not successful. Later, a toy manufacturer thought the material would make a good child's novelty item!

16. **True.** It's about 75 to 100 tons too heavy!

17. **True**

18. **True**

19. **True.** They didn't have any soap, and urine is alkaline—the opposite of acid.

20. **False.** This did happen, but they were listening to Wells's *War of the Worlds*.

21. **False.** Persians invented the Baghdad Battery about 2,000 years ago. It is a clay jar with an iron tube surrounded by copper. When filled with vinegar, it produced about 1.1 volts of electricity, but no one knows what the ancient Persians did with it!

22. **True.** He was fined 50 pounds (£) and the hat was outlawed for several years.

23. **False.** It was actually British secret agents who disguised explosive devices as rats, soap, and bicycle pumps. They would have made James Bond proud!

24. **False.** The tunnels are actually old gypsum and limestone quarries where Parisians got the rocks to build Notre Dame and other famous buildings.

25. **True.** The limit is actually 2 inches (5 cm). But you can wear higher heels if you get a permit.

26. **False.** Napoleon actually stood at 5 feet 7 inches (1.7 m), which was an average height for men at the time.

27. **True.** The error was discovered by a college student at the University of Chicago.

28. **True.** The architect saw the red of the primer on the steel beams and thought it looked lovely with the surrounding hills, so he custom-made the orange hue.

29. **True.**

30. **True.** You sat on the seat and pushed your feet along the ground and then let it glide for a few feet before pushing off again.

Keep Your Hat On! pages 98–99

1. **True**
2. **b**
3. **c.** Actress Sarah Bernhardt often wore men's clothes to challenge male-orientated society, so wearing a man's hat expressed freedom.
4. **d**
5. **a**
6. **True.** Often, each feather told a particular story. The headdresses were symbols of courage.
7. **c**   8. **c**   9. **c**
10. **True**
11. **c**   12. **b**

Against the Odds, pages 100–101

1. **c**   2. **b**
3. **True.** Keller's teacher Anne Sullivan taught her. Keller went on to get a college degree and be a spokesperson for people with disabilities.
4. **d**
5. **False.** Earhart did fly across the Atlantic. However, she failed in her attempt to fly around the world. She and her plane went down and were never found.
6. **d**   7. **b**   8. **c**   9. **a**
10. **a.** Rudolph recovered from polio and eventually was able to walk and run.

Map Mania! Perfect Palaces, pages 102–103

1. **b**   2. **c**   3. **c**   4. **b**
5. **d**   6. **a**   7. **1A**   8. **2E**
9. **3F**   10. **4C**   11. **5D**   12. **6B**

Game Show: Ultimate History Challenge, pages 104–105

1. **True**
2. **c**   3. **c**   4. **b**

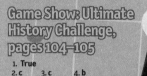

5. **True.** Researchers are training pigeons to recognize orange and yellow life jackets. Because pigeons are able to see color, including the ultraviolet bands, they are quicker and more reliable at locating survivors at sea than humans are.
6. **b**   7. **a**
8. **c.** A milliner is a person who makes hats.
9. **False.** She won two Nobel Prizes but for Chemistry and Physics.
10. **c**   11. **c**
12. **True.** In the Greek play *Oedipus Rex*, Oedipus becomes king of Thebes because he solves the riddle: What starts out on four legs, goes to two legs, and finishes on three? (Answer: a human being. People begin crawling on all fours, then walk on two legs, and may need the assistance of a cane, the "third leg," in old age.)
13. **a**   14. **d**   15. **d.**

SCORING

0–47

LIVING "NOW"

Your knowledge is up to the minute but a bit rusty on things that happened long ago. Consider visiting a museum or speaking with an older person who lived through history.

48–98

INTO THE FUTURE

You know that history repeats itself. The more you know about the past, the easier it is to understand the present, and sometimes to predict the future. So keep investigating history and have fun!

99–143

MAKING HISTORY

Time traveling is your life! You have an expert's sense of history. You love digging up interesting facts from the past. Who knows? You may make history yourself someday. Soon you'll be time traveling to the past and picking up juicy information along the way!

Number CRUNCHER

At the Ballgame, pages 108–109

1. c 2. b
3. b. In England and other countries soccer is called football.
4. False. The record was set by Seattle Seahawks football fans in 2013 at Centurylink Stadium in Seattle, Washington, U.S.A.
5. a 6. b
7. True. The scale of the giant model is 1 to 20 million, with the "planets" spread throughout the city of Stockholm and the country of Sweden.
8. c 9. c 10. a
11. True. It's a tradition of the Maori people, and the dance was originally performed before battle.
12. a

Great Wall, pages 110–111

1. True. Some sections were later connected.
2. b, some 1,800 years later.
3. c
4. False. The towers were used to watch for enemies and hold troops.
5. c 6. d 7. a 8. b 9. b
10. False. This has been a myth for a long time, but NASA believes it is nearly impossible to see the wall from the International Space Station with the naked eye.
11. c 12. a
13. True. For people who don't want to run so far, they also offer a half marathon and a 5.2-mile (8.4-km) "fun run."

Two Can Play That Game, pages 112–113

1. c
2. True. English boxing teacher Jack Broughton called them "mufflers."
3. b 4. c 5. a 6. b 7. c
8. False. The opposite is true: Olympic handball involves two teams of seven players, and the game is a little like soccer but players use their hands to carry the ball instead of kicking it with their feet.
9. a 10. b 11. b
12. True. As you throw darts at the board, you subtract the points you hit from the total.

True or False? Numbers in Nature, pages 114–115

1. True. Spiders have four pairs of jointed legs.
2. False. Ants, like most insects, have six legs.
3. False. That height and record belong to a redwood tree named "Hyperion" also in California.
4. True. Well-preserved fossils of jellyfish were found in Utah, U.S.A., and were dated back about 500 million years.
5. False. Covering 375,291 square miles (972,000 sq km), Greenland's National Park is a bit smaller than Egypt's 386,875 square miles (1,002,000 sq km). It is the world's largest national park.
6. True. Human eyes would have to be the size of baseballs to be the same proportion!
7. True. This was declared in 2002, the International Year of Mountains.
8. False. Chimpanzees are found in 21 African countries, mostly in the rain forests near the equator.
9. False. It is the world's largest flower, but it only grows to 3 feet (1 m) across.
10. True. But it doesn't sit still; it keeps moving thanks to our water cycle.
11. True. Water is also found in rivers and lakes, ice caps and glaciers, in the air, in the ground, and in animals … including us!
12. False. Snakes generally shed their skin three times a year.
13. True. They'll also piggyback on one another to conserve energy when moving.
14. False. It takes a couple of days.
15. True. The plants settled in layers at the bottom of swamps, which compressed into coal over the years.
16. True. The noises are used for everything from calling a mate to announcing that they're hungry.
17. True. When we see a rainbow we are actually seeing light bounce off raindrops.
18. False. Not quite; they're pregnant for up to two years.
19. True. Much of Mauna Loa lies under the sea. The volcano has erupted 33 times since 1843.
20. False. The amount is correct, but the location is Mawsynram, Meghalaya, India.
21. False. They cover about one-fifth of Earth's surface.
22. True. But scientists don't know the purpose of three of the eyes!
23. True. Earthquakes happen most frequently west of the Rocky Mountains.
24. False. Cheetahs are born with all their spots.
25. False. Eels can actually generate a burst of 600 volts, which is five times that of a wall socket.
26. True. But that's nothing compared to the Sami people of Scandinavia and Russia, who have at least 180 words for snow and ice.
27. False. The opposite is true.
28. False. Owls can turn their heads 270 degrees.
29. True. Many deer shed their antlers in winter. They generally begin growing back in the spring.
30. True. The wind speed was recorded by radar on March 5, 1999, in Bridge Creek, Oklahoma.

Nine to Five, pages 116–117

1. c
2. c
3. True. Men dominated the nursing field worldwide until well into the 1800s.
4. c
5. b, 4,270,550 employed.
6. d.
7. a
8. True. The hat is also known as a "toque blanche."
9. d. More than 60 hours a week.
10. b
11. b
12. c
13. True. International soccer stars Ronaldinho and Neymar were both paid more than this when they played for Brazilian team Santos.

Map Mania! Monumental Numbers, pages 118–119

1. b 2. c 3. a 4. c 5. b
6. a 7. 1C 8. 2E 9. 3A 10. 4F
11. 5B 12. 6D

Game Show: Ultimate Number Challenge, pages 120–121

1. False. As of 2013, the Federal Aviation Administration (FAA) requires new airline pilots to have at least 1,500 hours of flight time.
2. c 3. b 4. a 5. c
6. b 7. a 8. b 9. c
10. True. Ships need to be careful!
11. c
12. True. They're numbered 1 (I) to 76 (LXXVI).
13. b 14. c

SCORING

0–35

CONFUSED OR JUST PUZZLED?

You find number crunching a grind and mental math a headache, but you're prepared to figure things out. Try sudoku puzzles and trivia games to make your math skills soar.

36–72

COUNTING MACHINE

Calculus, logarithms, algebra, and trigonometry are probably a bit tricky, but you are mentally agile and quick with division and multiplication. You can impress your friends with facts and figures.

73–106

MEMORY STICK

You love memorizing trivia. You can remember your friends' birthdays, favorite colors, phone numbers, and addresses. Your head is filled with data. Your noggin is awash with numbers. You're a mathemagician!

Down to a SCIENCE

To the Moon, pages 124–125

1. b   2. b   3. b
4. a   5. d   6. c
7. **False.** After the launch, the spacecraft separated from the much larger rocket. The spacecraft consisted of the lunar module and the lunar lander.
8. c
9. **True.** Gravity on the moon is much weaker than on Earth. On the moon, you weigh less and can therefore jump higher.
10. a
11. **True.** Spacecraft have filmed the "dark side" of the moon, so we do know what it looks like!
12. c   13. d   14. b   15. c

Food for Thought, pages 126–127

1. c   2. c
3. **True.** Acorns were once an important part of many Native Americans' diets.
4. a   5. d   6. b   7. b   8. c

9. c
10. **True.** A red dye made from cochineal bugs colors many foods and cosmetics.
11. d   12. a

Brainbox, pages 128–129

1. d   2. b   3. a
4. **True.** The brain sends and receives pain signals from the rest of your body, though.
5. d   6. a   7. c
8. **False.** People and animals with larger bodies tend to have bigger brains, too—but the extra size doesn't make them smarter!
9. c   10. d   11. b   12. b   13. c
14. **False.** Even when you're resting, a brain scan will show activity throughout your entire brain.
15. b

On the Move, pages 130–131

1. d   2. c   3. d   4. a   5. a
6. b   7. b   8. b   9. a   10. d
11. d   12. c

True or False? Water Works, pages 132–133

1. **False.** The chemical formula for water is H_2O, or two hydrogen atoms and one oxygen atom.

2. **False.** The Mariana Trench is 36,201 feet (11,034 m) deep, and Everest is 29,035 feet (8,850 m) tall.
3. **False.** A person resting out of the sun could survive about a week with no water.
4. **True.** Lake Baikal is also the largest and oldest lake in the world.
5. **True.** But the baby must swim to the surface to breathe right after birth.
6. **True.** Volcanoes also spew out other gases from deep inside the earth.
7. **False.** Water also leaves the body when we breathe and sweat.
8. **True.** Freshwater contains minerals in addition to H_2O that give it the flavor we're used to.

9. **False.** Cows use up more water per pound than sheep, pigs, goats, or chickens.
10. **True.** Water that falls to the ground in any form is called precipitation.
11. **True.** Mercury may be the hottest planet, but ice lurks in shaded areas near the poles.
12. **False.** Alligators breathe through their nostrils, which stay above the surface while the rest of their body is underwater.

13. **False.** While it's falling, the bottom of a raindrop flattens until it looks like a hamburger bun.
14. **True.** Lots of water is formed when stars are born.
15. **False.** No rain has fallen in the Dry Valleys of Antarctica for 2 million years.
16. **True.** A one-year-old baby's body is about 65 percent water, while an adult woman's is about 55 percent.
17. **True.** Chemicals from the paint could end up in lakes, rivers, or oceans.
18. **True.** However, in wealthy countries, air pollution leads to more deaths each year.
19. **False.** River otters used to be hunted for their fur, but the population is now healthy and growing.
20. **True.** Oceans contain about 96.5 percent of Earth's water!
21. **True.** Chlorine combines with sweat and sunscreen to cause that funny "pool smell."
22. **False.** Groundwater slowly seeps along through soil and around rocks and often makes its way to rivers or lakes.
23. **False.** Most jellyfish do not sting, but don't touch an unknown jellyfish, just in case!
24. **False.** No fish live in the Dead Sea, but scientists have found bacteria living in the salty water.
25. **True.** A rock called a hydrous mineral contains water in its chemical structure.
26. **True.** Starfish eyes form very simple images—the starfish has no brain!
27. **False.** San Francisco, California, U.S.A., is the first city taking steps to ban plastic water bottles.
28. **True.** The acid rain never reaches the surface—it evaporates back into the clouds as it falls.
29. **True.** Many African villages don't have running water. It's mainly the responsibility of women to go get water.
30. **False.** The total amount of water on Earth stays the same, but the number of people who need water is increasing.

Medical Matters, pages 134–135
1. c
2. **False.** In childhood, the appendix produces hormones that control body systems. In adulthood, it helps the body fight off germs and diseases.
3. b   4. c   5. a   6. b
7. **True.** Toeprints are as unique as fingerprints and have been used to identify criminals.
8. c   9. d
10. **False.** Just 4 to 6 percent of kids are allergic to a food, such as milk, eggs, or peanuts.
11. **True.** In the 1830s, doctors believed that removing blood from the body could cure diseases.
12. a   13. c
14. **True.** A child with a broken bone needs to see a doctor quickly so the bone can be positioned properly before it begins to heal.

Can You Hear Me Now? pages 136–137
1. a   2. c   3. a   4. b   5. c
6. **True.** In 1861, a German inventor, Johann Philipp Reis, made a kind of telephone using parts of a beer barrel, a sausage skin, and a piece of platinum metal.

7. c   8. a   9. b   10. b   11. d
12. **False.** A device called the Alpha UWCP allows divers to make calls via Bluetooth from under the water.

Map Mania! Destinations in Danger, pages 138–139
1. a   2. c   3. b   4. a
5. b   6. d   7. 1F   8. 2D
9. 3E   10. 4B   11. 5A   12. 6C

Game Show: Ultimate Science Challenge, pages 140–141
1. d
2. **True.** Instead, jellyfish have a simple network of nerves.
3. c   4. b   5. c   6. a   7. b
8. **False.** But dogs went to space before people did! A dog from Russia named Laika was the first living creature to orbit Earth.
9. **True.** The moon gets up to 417°F (214°C)!
10. d   11. c   12. d
13. a   14. a   15. c

SCORING

0–45
SCIENCE SHY
You're a creative free spirit who likely loves art or reading, but science freaks you out a bit. Believe it or not, scientists are fun and creative, too! Read about black holes or search for artsy experiments online.

46–92
BRAIN STORM
You're full of ideas and you're not afraid to get out there and experiment, but you rush through things sometimes. Start going step by step and you'll become a great chemist one day. Make sure you experiment wisely——and be safe out there!

93–137
REAL GENIUS
Have you ever taken an IQ test? You never know, you might score higher than Einstein! Put your genius and your mighty brains to work with a career in physics, math, or computer science. But don't forget to take your nose out of those equations to smell the roses sometimes.

Native Know-How, pages 144–145

1. d 2. b 3. b
4. c 5. a 6. a
7. **True.** The Mohawk was named after a hairstyle worn by male warriors of the Mohawk tribe.
8. c. Algonquin is a Native American language.
9. b 10. c
11. **True.** War chiefs, who were considered the bravest in the tribe, had the most feathers in their headdress.
12. a 13. a 14. b

Summer Survival Kit, pages 146–147

1. a
2. **True.** Sparklers can reach a temperature of 1800°F (982°C). The melting point of silver is 1763°F (962°C).
3. b 4. b 5. c 6. c
7. **False.** Poison ivy rashes are not contagious, but you should avoid touching any objects that have brushed against the ivy.
8. b 9. c 10. a 11. c
12. b 13. b

True or False? Going to Extremes, pages 148–149

1. **False.** As of 2012, researchers believe that Bolivia's Madidi National Park is the most biodiverse; it's home to 11 percent of the world's birds, more than 200 species of mammals, almost 300 types of fish, and some 12,000 different plants.
2. **False.** Though Baumgartner did achieve the highest skydive, he dove from a balloon capsule that was 24 miles (39 km) aboveground in Earth's stratosphere—the second layer of the atmosphere.
3. **True.** Arica received no rainfall between October 1903 and January 1918.
4. **False.** With 130 active volcanoes, Indonesia is the country with the most active volcanoes in the world.
5. **True.** Bungee jumping traces its roots to Vanuatu, an island nation in the South Pacific, where people still celebrate the harvest by tying vines to their ankles and diving from towers.
6. **True.** According to the Scoville scale, which measures chili-pepper heat, peppers such as habanero are more than 250 times hotter than the common jalapeño.
7. **False.** Lindbergh flew nonstop across the Atlantic Ocean—from New York to Paris—in 1927.
8. **True.** Though the rhinoceros beetle isn't large compared to most animals, it can move about 850 times its body weight.
9. **True.** The Nile River spans 4,132 miles (6,650 km), while the Mississippi River runs 2,340 miles (3,766 km).

10. **True.** The tornadoes occurred from April 27–28 in 2011.
11. **False.** The race took place in 1929 in North America, where runners started the race in New York City and ended 3,635 miles (5,850 km) away in Los Angeles.
12. **True.** Camels can survive for long periods without eating because they can use fat stored in their humps for energy.
13. **False.** The International Space Station takes about 90 minutes to orbit Earth. That's about 16 times a day.
14. **True.** Scientists have even identified a 300-million-year-old cockroach ancestor that existed before the age of dinosaurs.
15. **True.** Some sand dunes are 1,000 feet (300 m) tall, while the Eiffel Tower is 902 feet (275 m) tall.
16. **False.** Although Michigan Stadium is so large that it can seat 109,901 people, it is not visible from space.
17. **True.** In fact, swimming pools inspired the design of half-pipes.
18. **True.** Jupiter's giant red spot is a storm that has lasted for at least 340 years.
19. **True.** The Maya believed the sacrifice would strengthen society and please the gods.
20. **False.** Although iceberg B-15 wasn't as large as Texas, it measured 4,250 square miles (11,007 sq km)—almost the size of Connecticut, U.S.A.
21. **True.** Heyerdahl wanted to prove that people in South America could have built rafts and sailed to Polynesia before the time of Columbus.
22. **True.** The shortfin mako shark can make such a tall leap when traveling at a speed of 24.6 miles an hour (39.6 km/h).
23. **True.** In 1960, Don Walsh and Jacques Piccard traveled 35,840 feet (10,924 m) beneath the ocean surface aboard the deep-sea submersible *Trieste*. In 2012, *Titanic* and *Avatar* director James Cameron made the same journey aboard a submersible he helped design.
24. **False.** The hole was 8 miles (12.9 km) deep, while the distance to the center of Earth is about 4,000 miles (6,437 km).
25. **True.** The average temperature on Venus is 863°F (462°C), and the melting point of lead is 621.5°F (327.5°C).
26. **False.** People from all social classes surfed.
27. **True.** The Seven Summits include Mount Kilimanjaro in Africa, Mount Kosciuszko in Australia, Mount Elbrus in Europe, Aconcagua in South America, Mount McKinley in North America, Mount Vinson in Antarctica, and Mount Everest in Asia.

28. **True.** According to Guinness World Records, Knievel had 433 bone fractures, which included broken arms, hips, and ribs.

29. **False.** The blue whale, which weighs about 200 tons (181,437 kg), can eat up to 8 tons (7,257 kg) of krill in a single day.
30. **True.** Webb covered himself in porpoise oil to decrease drag. It took him about 22 hours to swim across the channel.

Awesome Australia, pages 150–151

1. b 2. a
3. **True.** In 2013, there were about 23 million people living in Australia compared to 74 million sheep.
4. b 5. c 6. b 7. d
8. **True.** Before the American Revolution, the English sent their prisoners to the American Colonies. But after the United States won its independence in 1776, the criminals were sent to Australia.
9. b 10. a 11. b
12. c 13. b 14. a

Odd Sports, pages 152–153

1. b
2. **False.** Sumo wrestlers win by either pushing their opponent outside the ring or making their opponent touch the ground with any body part except the soles of the feet.
3. d 4. d 5. a 6. c
7. b 8. c 9. a
10. **True.** For 40 years, Olympic medals were awarded for painting, sculpture, architecture, literature, and music.
11. b 12. a 13. c

Map Mania! On Safari, pages 154–155

1. c 2. b 3. a 4. b 5. d
6. a 7. d 8. 1D 9. 2F 10. 3A
11. 4B 12. 5E 13. 6G 14. 7C

Game Show: Ultimate Adventure Challenge pages 156–157

1. c
2. **False.** The sport is named for the sled's bony appearance.
3. **True.** The ride, located in Six Flags Great Adventure in New Jersey, U.S.A., is 415 feet (126 m) tall, while the Statue of Liberty stands 305 feet (93 m) tall.
4. d 5. d 6. b 7. c
8. **False.** Commonly used in the African language Swahili, "safari" does indeed come from an Arabic word but simply meaning journey not hunt.
9. c 10. b 11. d 12. d
13. **False.** In 1963, Russian cosmonaut Valentina Tereshkova was the first woman to travel into space.
14. b

169

SCORING

0–38
STARTING FROM SCRATCH
You may have started with a clean sheet, but you're gaining marks and climbing up. Take it one step at a time and you'll soon reach the top.

39–76
LEARNING NEW TRICKS
Exploration and discovery excite you. You're finding new ways of working things out. If you get sidetracked, think outside the box and find a new adventure to chase!

77–112
ADVENTURE EXPERT
Your knowledge and sense of adventure know no bounds. Keep up your adventurous spirit, daredevil attitude, and can-do spirit. But be careful out there! Your enthusiasm and drive will take you as far as you want to go. Take each challenge as it comes.

GRAND TALLY

Having worked your way through *Quiz Whiz 5*, is your brain all chewed up? Or are you now Top Dog of quizzes? Tally your scores from all eight chapters to learn how you stack up against other brainiacs. Use the chart to find out your *Quiz Whiz* status.

0–345
TRIVIA NOVICE
A novice is someone new to a job, someone who has yet to learn the skills and techniques needed to succeed. With this *Quiz Whiz* score, you are on a learning curve and have a good way to go, but you have the desire to improve. Try a variety of quizzes and puzzles, and test your knowledge whenever you can. "Practice makes perfect" is a traditional saying based on reality: The more books, magazines, and newspapers you read—whether in print or online—the more your brain cells will work for you and fill your memory banks. Much of the information you read will soak in and take you to the next level.

346–690
APPRENTICE
You've clearly learned the art and science of remembering facts and figures, but now you need to take on new challenges and set higher goals. There's lots more to learn to be a quiz champion!

691–1,034
THE WHIZ OF QUIZ
You're the front-runner, the leader of the pack of *Quiz Whiz* challengers! Continue to use your animal intelligence, well-trained brain, and dogged determination to be the best in everything you do.

Pop Culture [52–65]

52-53, [BKGD], Disney/Pixar/TF; 54 [UP], The Granger Collection/TF; 54 [CTR], 2005/TF; 54 [LO], United Archives/TF; 55 [UP], WALT DISNEY PICTURES/KC; 55 [LO], Warner Bros/TF; 56-57 [BKGD], robert_s/SS; 60 [UP], lambada/GI; 60 [LO], StepStock/SS; 61 [UP], Kevingrotz/DRMS; 61 [LO], Sharifphoto/DRMS; 63 [BKGD], DREAMWORKS ANIMATION/MAD HATTER ENTERTAINMENT/KC; 64 [CTR], Alptraum/DRMS; 64 [LO], Jiripravda/DRMS; 65 [UP], PAISAN HOMHUAN/SS; 65 [CTR], Carrienelson1/DRMS; 65 [LO-A], Cyanidsyd/DRMS; 65 [LO-B], jfmdesign/IS; 65 [LO-C], Radub85/DRMS; 65 [LO-D], Radub85/DRMS.

Back to Nature [66–83]

66-67 [BKGD], redswept/SS; 66 [UP], Emily Starbuck Crone/DRMS; 67 [UP], Patrick Poendl/DRMS; 67 [CTR], Brett Critchley/DRMS; 68-69 [BKGD], Tomatito26/DRMS; 70 [UP], Solarseven/DRMS; 70 [CTR], Eric Lundberg/DRMS; 70 [LO], Alhovik/DRMS; 71 [UP], Andres Rodriguez/DRMS; 71 [LO], Ryszard Laskowski/DRMS; 72-73 [BKGD], biletskiy/SS; 74 [1], Joerg Habermeier/DRMS; 74 [2], Dirk Ercken/DRMS; 74 [3], Dawid Ba_uch/DRMS; 75 [4], Nilanjan Bhattacharya/DRMS; 75 [5], Seawhisper/DRMS; 75 [6], Sean Pavone/DRMS; 76 [UP], Eric Isselee/SS; 76 [CTR], Vetre Antanaviciute-meskauskiene/DRMS; 76 [LO], Mike2focus/DRMS; 77 [UP], Hlnicaise/DRMS; 77 [CTR], Emily2k/DRMS; 77 [LO], L Hill/DRMS; 80-81 [BKGD], Ethel Davies/RH; 82 [CTR], Jolanta Mazus/DRMS; 82 [LO], Skydie/DRMS; 83 [UP], Andrew Emptage/DRMS; 83 [UP-A], Nevinates/DRMS; 83 [UP-B], Flynt/DRMS; 83 [UP-C], Holly Kuchera/DRMS; 83 [UP-D], Isselee/DRMS; 83 [CTR LE], Martine De Graaf/DRMS; 83 [CTR RT], Dpimborough/DRMS.

The Rest is History [84–105]

84-85 [BKGD], Sphinx Wang/SS; 86 [UP], Abxyz/DRMS; 86 [LO LE], Chris Dorney/DRMS; 86 [LO RT], ITAR-TASS/TF; 87 [UP], The Print Collector/HIP/TF; 87 [LO], The Granger Collection/TF; 88-89 [BKGD], Doug Scott/age fotostock/RH; 90 [UP], RIA Novosti/TF; 90 [CTR], Isselee/DRMS; 90 [LO], Leonello Calvetti /DRMS; 91 [UP], Erik Lam/SS; 91 [LO LE], Isselee/DRMS; 91 [LO RT], Splosh/DRMS; 92-93 [BKGD], Kwiatek7/SS; 94-95 [BKGD], Africa Studio/SS; 098 [UP], Alexander Makhal/DRMS; 098 [LO], Photo25th/DRMS; 099 [UP], Katrina Brown/DRMS; 099 [CTR], Vvoevale/DRMS; 099 [LO],National Pictures/TF; 100-101 [BKGD], TF; 102 [1], Bjeayes/DRMS; 102 [2], Hou Guima/DRMS; 102 [3], Dan Breckwoldt/DRMS; 103 [4], Olgarakhm/DRMS; 103 [5], Sergiu Marian Leustean/DRMS; 103 [6], Dennis Dolkens/DRMS; 104 [CTR LE], Paul B. Moore/SS; 104 [CTR RT], Wollertz/DRMS; 104 [LO], Gale Verhague/DRMS; 105 [UP], Speedfighter17/DRMS; 105 [LO LE], Tracy Whiteside/DRMS; 105 [LO-A], Ijansempoi/DRMS; 105 [LO-B], Katrina Brown/DRMS; 105 [LO-C], Dvmsimages/DRMS; 105 [LO-D], Yuriy Chaban/DRMS.

Number Cruncher [106–121]

106-107 [BKGD], James Boardman/DRMS; 108 [UP], Baibaz/DRMS; 108 [CTR], Andrew

Barker/DRMS; 108 [LO], Mira Agron/DRMS; 109 [UP], Cynthia Farmer/DRMS; 109 [LO],
Thomas Northcut/GI; 110-111 [BKGD], Luoxubin/DRMS; 112[UP], Py2000/DRMS; 112[CTR],
Phil Cole/GI; 112[LO], Les Cunliffe/DRMS; 113[UP], Poznyakov/DRMS; 113[LO], Bjørn
Hovdal/DRMS; 116-117 [BKGD], Gergely Zsolnai/DRMS; 118 [1], Piero Cruciatti/DRMS;
118 [2], Crackerclips/DRMS; 118 [3], Silvian Tomescu/DRMS; 119 [4], Josemaria Toscano/
DRMS; 119 [5], Simon Gurney/DRMS; 119 [6], Suzib_100/DRMS; 120 [UP], Xi Zhang/DRMS;
120 [CTR LE], wizdata/SS; 120 [LO LE], Isselee/DRMS; 120 [LO RT], Gennaro86/DRMS;
121 [UP], Peter Sobolev/DRMS; 121 [CTR RT], Alexandre Dvihally/DRMS; 121 [LO-A], Arno
Meintjes/DRMS; 121 [LO-B], Viorel Sima/DRMS; 121 [LO-C], Joanne Weston/DRMS; 121
[LO-D], Photographerlondon/DRMS.

Down to a Science [122–141]
122-123 [BKGD], Monkey Business Images/SS; 124-125 [BKGD], The Granger Collection/
TF; 126 [UP], Nevinates/DRMS; 126 [CTR], Valentyn Volkov/SS; 126 [LO], Eric Isselee/SS;
127 [UP], Yuangeng Zhang/SS; 127 [CTR], Hong Vo/SS; 127 [LO], Jennifer Barrow/DRMS;
128-129 [BKGD], pogonici/SS; 130 [UP], Philippilosian/DRMS; 130 [CTR], Toa555/DRMS;
130 [LO], Gunold Brunbauer/DRMS; 131 [UP], Per Björkdahl/DRMS; 131 [LO], Bennymarty/
DRMS; 134-135 [BKGD], Photomo/DRMS; 136 [UP], Elena Duvernay/DRMS; 136 [LO], /
GI; 137 [UP], Andreblais/DRMS; 137 [CTR], Robnroll/SS; 137 [LO], Serrnovik/DRMS; 138
[1], Jonmilnes/DRMS; 138 [2], Edwardshtern/DRMS; 138 [3], Kira Kaplinski/DRMS; 139
[4], Betsy Verb/DRMS; 139 [5], Sergey Uryadnikov/DRMS; 139 [6], Swisshippo/DRMS;
140 [CTR LE], Kutt Niinepuu/DRMS; 140 [CTR RT], Dmitriy Shironosov/DRMS; 140 [LO],
Vaclav Volrab/DRMS; 141 [UP], William Moneymaker/DRMS; 141 [CTR LE], H.ARMSTRONG
ROBERTS/ClassicStock/TF; 141 [CTR RT], Penywise/DRMS; 141 [LO-A], Timothy Epp/
DRMS; 141 [LO-B], Anna Sedneva/DRMS; 141 [LO-C], Irochka/DRMS; 141 [LO-D], Edyta
Pawlowska/DRMS.

World of Adventure [142–157]
142-143 [BKGD], Maxim Blinkov/SS; 144 [UP], Verena Matthew/DRMS; 144 [CTR],
Johnfoto/DRMS; 144 [LO], Darren Brode/DRMS; 145 [UP], Shannon Fagan/DRMS;
145 [CTR], American Spirit/SS; 145 [LO], Geoff Brightling/GI; 146-147 [BKGD], Kjersti
Joergensen/SS; 150-151 [BKGD], Stanislav Fosenbauer/SS; 152 [UP], Brad Sauter/DRMS;
152 [LO], Herbert Kratky/SS; 153 [UP], Steve Heap/SS; 153 [CTR], Flynt/DRMS; 153 [LO],
Jennifer Russell/DRMS; 154 [1], Matthew Amery/DRMS; 154 [2], Palko72/DRMS; 154 [3],
Javarman/DRMS; 154 [4], Peter.wey/DRMS; 155 [5], Walter Quirtmair/DRMS; 155 [6],
Awcnz62/DRMS; 155 [7], Jason Prince/DRMS; 156 [CTR LE], Sergey Skleznev/DRMS; 156
[CTR RT], Sculpies/DRMS; 157 [UP], Reinhardt/DRMS; 157 [CTR-A], Chin Kit Sen/SS; 157
[CTR-B], Erik Lam/DRMS; 157 [CTR-C], Putnik/DRMS; 157 [CTR-D], Erik Lam/DRMS; 157
[CTR RT], Shi Yali/SS; 157 [LO-A], Stephen Noakes/DRMS; 157 [LO-B], Mike2focus/DRMS;
157 [LO-C], torsten kuenzlen/DRMS; 157 [LO-D], Thyrymn/DRMS.

Staff for This book
Priyanka Sherman and Amy Briggs, *Project Editors*
Julide Dengel, *Associate Art Director*
Kelley Miller, *Senior Photo Editor*
Carl Mehler, *Director of Maps*
Vanessa Mack, *Associate Photo Editor*
Angela Modany, Paige Towler, *Editorial Assistants*
Erica Holsclaw, *Special Projects Assistant*
Sanjida Rashid, *Design Production Assistant*
Michael Cassady, *Rights Clearance Specialist*
Grace Hill, *Managing Editor*
Mike O'Connor, *Production Editor*
Lewis R. Bassford, *Production Manager*
Darrick McRae, *Manager, Production Services*
Susan Borke, *Legal and Business Affairs*

Published by the National Geographic Society
Gary E. Knell, *President and CEO*
John M. Fahey, *Chairman of the Board*
Melina Gerosa Bellows, *Chief Education Officer*
Declan Moore, *Chief Media Officer*
Hector Sierra, *Senior Vice President and General
    Manager, Book Division*

**Editorial, Design, and Production by
    Bender Richardson White**
Nancy Honovich, Alicia Klepeis, Kathryn Hulick
    Gargolinksi, Jack Silbert, Jeri Cipriano, Karina
    Hamalainen, *Contributors*

**Senior Management Team, Kids Publishing and
    Media**
Nancy Laties Feresten, *Senior Vice President*
Jennifer Emmett, *Vice President, Editorial Director,
    Kids Books*
Julie Vosburgh Agnone, *Vice President, Editorial
    Operations*
Rachel Buchholz, *Editor and Vice President*, NG
    Kids *magazine*
Michelle Sullivan, *Vice President, Kids Digital*
Eva Absher-Schantz, *Design Director*
Jay Sumner, *Photo Director*
Hannah August, *Marketing Director*
R. Gary Colbert, *Production Director*

Digital
Anne McCormack, *Director*
Laura Goertzel, Sara Zeglin, *Producers*
Jed Winer, *Special Projects Assistant*
Emma Rigney, *Creative Producer*
Brian Ford, *Video Producer*
Bianca Bowman, *Assistant Producer*
Natalie Jones, *Senior Product Manager*

For more information, please visit
nationalgeographic.com, call 1-800-NGS LINE
(647-5463), or write to the following address:

National Geographic Society
1145 17th Street N.W.
Washington, D.C. 20036-4688 U.S.A.

Visit us online at
nationalgeographic.com/books

For librarians and teachers:
ngchildrensbooks.org

More for kids from National Geographic:
kids.nationalgeographic.com

For information about special discounts for
bulk purchases, please contact National
Geographic Books Special Sales:
ngspecsales@ngs.org

For rights or permissions inquiries, please
contact National Geographic Books Subsidiary
Rights: ngbookrights@ngs.org

Paperback ISBN: 978-1-4263-1907-5
Reinforced library binding: 978-1-4263-1908-2

Printed in the United States of America
15/QGT-CML/1

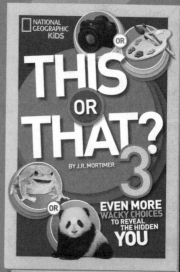